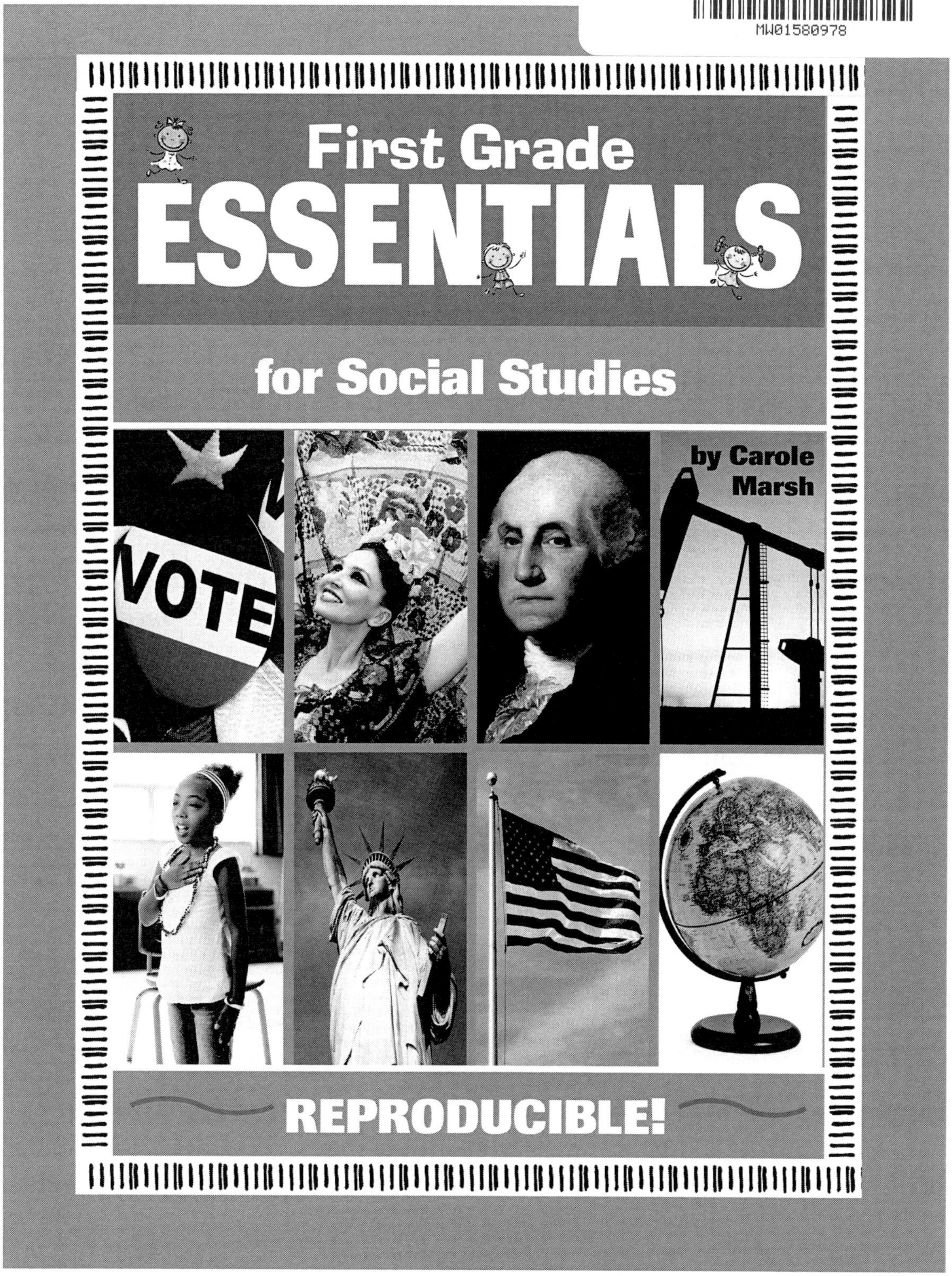

First Grade ESSENTIALS
for Social Studies

by Carole Marsh

REPRODUCIBLE!

©2017 Carole Marsh/Gallopade/Peachtree City, GA • All Rights Reserved
Published by Gallopade • Manufactured in the USA
Current Edition ©December 2019

Dear Teachers,

Have you ever wished you had everything you needed to teach social studies in one easy-to-use resource? Now you have it in *First Grade Essentials for Social Studies*. Even in first grade, students are expected to learn a lot! This book will help you meet essential state standards with age-appropriate activities in a fun, attractive, and interesting style!

In addition to almost 100 reproducible activity pages, this book offers even more hands-on learning opportunities with templates, graphic organizers, writing prompts, project-based learning ideas, and vocabulary cards with definitions. The writing prompts and vocabulary cards are designed so you can cut them out individually. You can mix and match these "extras" to topics you are studying, to activity pages in the book, or use them on their own.

What is my goal with this book? I want to make your life easier as you introduce your students to the social studies topics and skills they absolutely need to know. I am confident this book accomplishes exactly that!

From my desk to yours,

[signature]

Your First Grade Essentials are already attractive and fun (in addition to educational, of course), but you can customize them to make them colorful and unique!

Copy Writing Prompts and Vocabulary Cards onto colored paper. Choose colors that match your classroom decorative theme, a theme for social studies materials, or use an assortment of colors. Or, as an alternative, copy them onto white paper, and use your markers, highlighters, stickers, and glitter-glue to add personalization and pizzazz to the borders. Either way, laminate them so they last!

P.S. I would LOVE to see what you come up with! Connect with me at Gallopade on Facebook or Pinterest.

Table of Contents

Foundations

Days in a Week 5	Transportation Changes! 11
Weeks in a Month 6	Communities Change! 12
Months of the Year 7	Families Change! 13
Past and Present 8	Primary and Secondary Sources 14
Your Life! 9	Artifact Detective 15
Schools Change! 10	

History

Jamestown 16	Abraham Lincoln 22
Pocahontas 17	16th U.S. President 23
George Washington 18	George Washington Carver 24
First U.S. President 19	Great Scientist 25
Thomas Jefferson 20	Martin Luther King Jr. 26
Third U.S. President 21	Civil Rights Leader 27

Geography

What Maps Show 28	Continents 39
Globes Are Great! 29	Oceans 40
Shapes of Places 30	Our Nation's Capital! 41
Where Are We? 31	State Capitals 42
Maps Can Show Land 32	What is Geography? 43
Maps Can Show Water 33	Seasons Change! 44
Map Titles 34	Unique Features 45
Map Symbols 35	The Environment 46
Cardinal Directions 36	Geography Impacts Meeting Needs ... 47
Use a Compass Rose 37	Physical Surroundings Affect Jobs 48
Make Your Own Map! 38	

Economics

- Goods Are Good 49
- Services Are Special 50
- Producers and Consumers 51
- We Consume and Produce 52
- Scarcity 53
- Costs and Benefits 54
- Let's Trade! 55
- Money! 56
- Making Choices 57
- Now or Later? 58
- Spend or Save? 59

Civics

- My Community's History 60
- Customs and Celebrations! 61
- Culture Changes 62
- Part of Many Groups 63
- A Diverse America! 64
- Common Traditions! 65
- Model Citizens 66
- Good Citizens 67
- Follow the Rules 68
- Responsible Citizens 69
- Good Citizens Work Hard! 70
- Good Citizens Vote! 71
- Volunteer! 72
- Vote for Leaders 73
- Symbols and Traditions 74
- Patriotism 75
- "America the Beautiful" 76
- "My Country 'Tis of Thee" 77
- American Flag 78
- Pledge of Allegiance 79
- The Statue of Liberty 80
- Liberty Bell 81
- Washington Monument 82
- Bald Eagle 83
- Star-Spangled Banner 84
- Independence Day 85
- Columbus Day 86
- Presidents' Day 87
- Martin Luther King Jr. Day 88
- New Year's Day 89
- Veterans Day 90
- Memorial Day 91
- Labor Day 92
- Yearly Traditions 93
- Our President 94

Appendix

- Graphic Organizers/Templates 95
- Writing Prompts 109
- Project-Based Learning 114
- Vocabulary 121

Days in a Week

There are seven **days** in a **week**.

They are Sunday, Monday, Tuesday, Wednesday, Thursday, Friday, and Saturday.

This calendar shows one week:

Calendar

Sunday	Monday	Tuesday	Wednesday	Thursday	Friday	Saturday
1	2	3	4	5	6	7

Complete these steps using the calendar above:
- **Say the days of the week out loud.**
- **Circle Sunday in yellow.**
- **Circle the day after Sunday in green.**
- **Circle Thursday in red.**
- **Circle the day before Thursday in blue.**

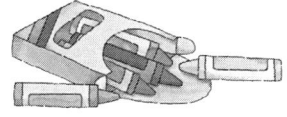

Which two days are considered to be the "weekend"?

_____   _____

Weeks in a Month

This calendar shows one **month**. Most months have four weeks, with a few days left over.

Calendar

Sunday	Monday	Tuesday	Wednesday	Thursday	Friday	Saturday
1	2	3	4	5	6	7
8	9	10	11	12	13	14
15	16	17	18	19	20	21
22	23	24	25	26	27	28
29	30	31				

Color each week of the calendar a different color.
Then answer the questions.

1. How many days are in each week? _____

2. How many days are in this month? _____

3. How many complete weeks are in this month? _____

4. How many days are left over in this month? _____

5. What month is it right now? _____

Months of the Year

There are 12 months in a year. They are:

1 January   2 February   3 March   4 April

5 May   6 June   7 July   8 August

9 September   10 October   11 November   12 December

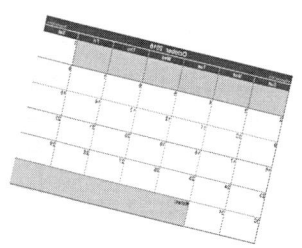

Use a calendar to study the months of the year. Answer these questions.

1. What month is the first month of the year?
   _____

2. How many months are in a year?
   _____

3. What month comes between June and August?
   _____

4. Fill in the blank: March, _____, May

5. What is the last month of the year?
   _____

Past and Present

People in the past lived differently than we do today. In the past, many men worked on farms and grew food for their families. They built their own houses. Women often helped on farms, cooked, and sewed clothes. Children worked on farms, too.

In the present, men and women have many different jobs to choose from. Most jobs are away from home. Families buy their food at stores and restaurants. A builder builds their houses. Families buy clothes at stores. Children go to school.

Match each picture from the past with the picture that what that action or place looks like in the present.

Past

Present

YOUR LIFE!

Chronological order describes the order events occurred.

When we write things down in the order they happened, we are putting them in chronological order.

Build your timeline!

Draw pictures of yourself in the past, present, and future.

Past   Present   Future

Remember When?

**Here are three events from your life.
Number them 1, 2, or 3 in the order they occurred.**

_____ I learned to walk.

_____ I began first grade.

_____ I went to kindergarten.

Schools Change!

Schools change over time.

In the past, many schools only had one room and one teacher. Students of all ages had class together. Children had to walk a long way to school. Students wrote on slate with chalk.

Today, schools have different classes for different ages. Children who live far away can ride a bus. Today, students have books, paper, and computers. Most students go to school much longer today too!

Look at the photographs. Then choose the best answer to each question.

School in the past

School today

1. Is the photograph of the school in the past a primary source?
   ___ yes   ___ no

2. Is the photograph of the school today a primary source?
   ___ yes   ___ no

3. What can you learn from these photographs?
   ___ Schools today are the same as schools in the past.
   ___ Schools today are a lot different from schools in the past.

Transportation Changes!

Transportation changes over time.

In the past, transportation was by horse, by wagon, by ship, or on foot.
Next, trains and steamboats became a faster way to travel.
Today people travel in cars and airplanes. Ships and trains quickly move food and goods. Subways and buses provide rides too.

Imagine the future...
Self-driving cars?   Solar cars?   Quick trips to Mars?

Draw what the car from the present might look like.

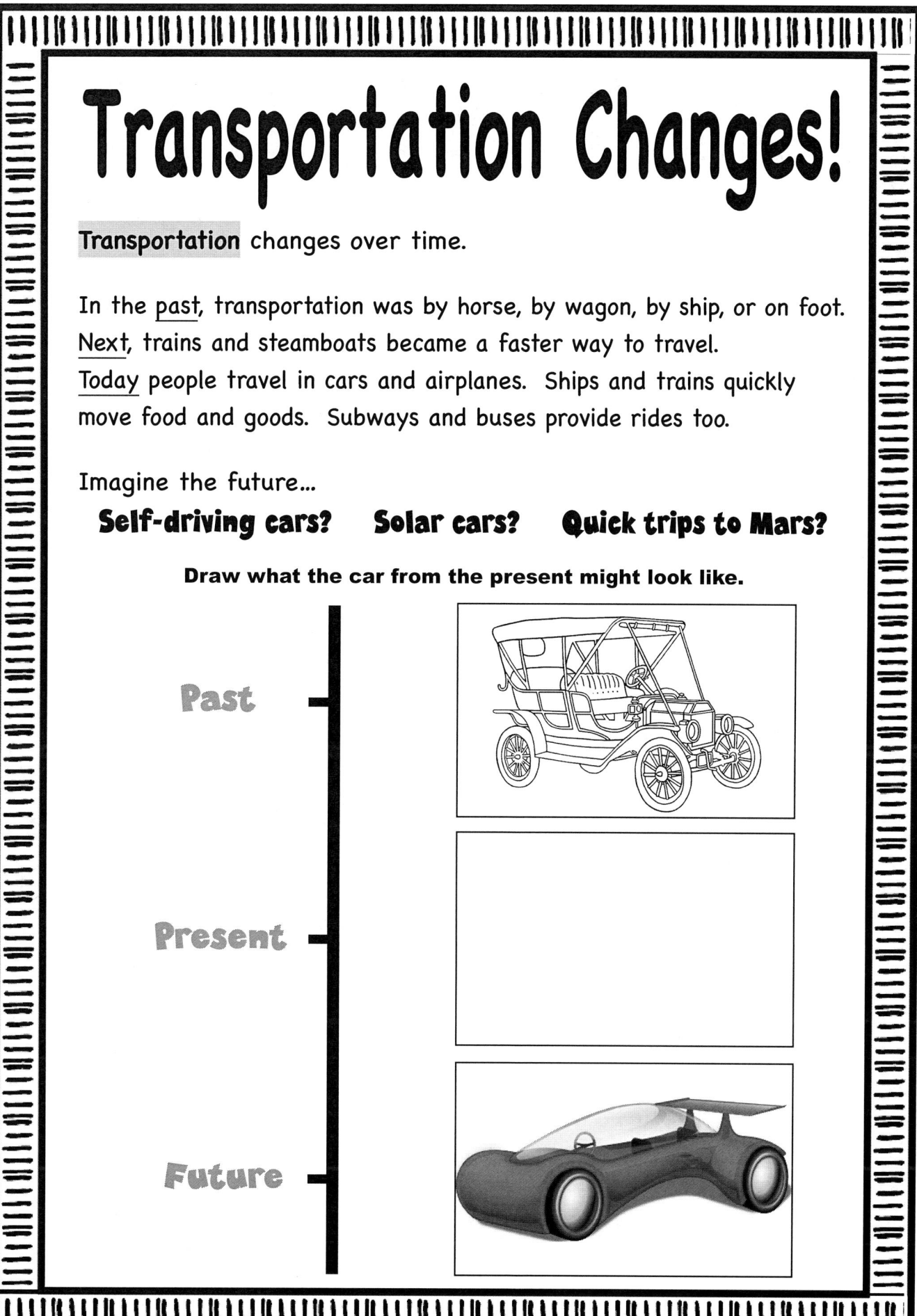

Communities Change!

Communities change over time.

In the past, communities were smaller. They had fewer people and fewer businesses. Communities did not provide many services.

Today, communities are larger. Some communities have huge populations. Some have tall buildings. Communities today provide many services like police and traffic lights and clean water.

Look at the physical and human features on the maps.
Write P under the map that shows Miller Town in the past.
Write T under the map that shows Miller Town today.

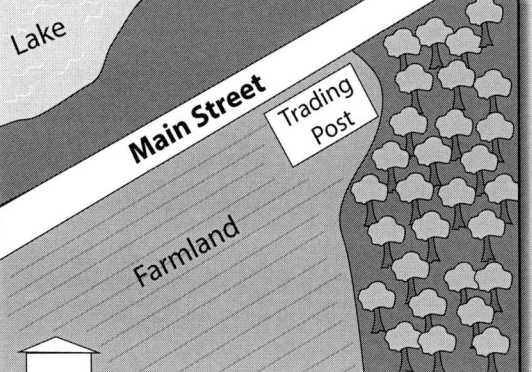
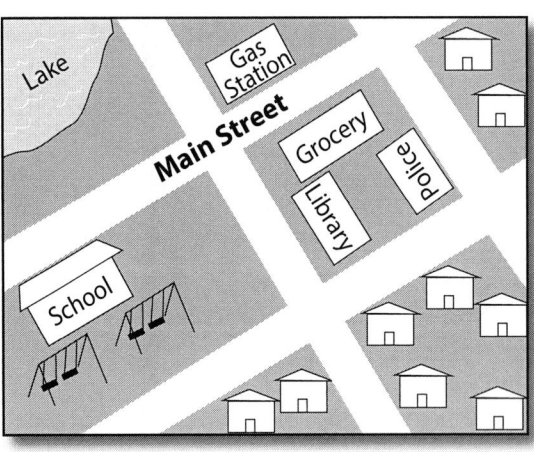

Describe how Miller Town changed over time.

_____
_____

Families Change!

Families change over time.

In the past, families made their own clothes and grew their own food. They did not have television or phones. Everyone worked hard to survive!

Today, families buy food and clothes in stores. They drive cars, talk on cellphones, and watch movies. Inventions make many family chores easier than in the past!

Label the pictures past and present.

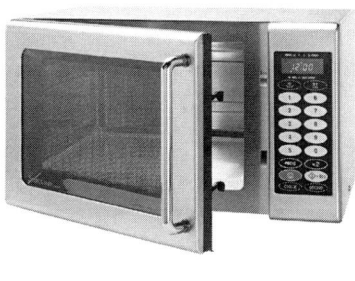

_____

Describe family life in the future. Be creative!

_____

_____

_____

PRIMARY AND SECONDARY SOURCES

As you study social studies topics, you will use primary sources and secondary sources to learn about people and events.

A **primary source** is a record of an event made by a person who was there when the event occurred. A primary source is original, "first-hand" information.

Examples of primary sources:

- photographs
- journals
- letters
- objects like clothing and tools

A **secondary source** is something created after an event by someone who was not there. It is not original information. A secondary source is "second-hand" information.

Examples of secondary sources:

- textbooks
- Internet articles
- encyclopedias
- magazine articles

Write P by each primary source.
Write S by each secondary source.

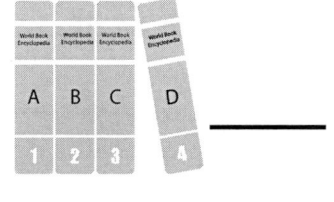

Artifact Detective

Artifacts are objects people used in the past.
An artifact is also a primary source.

Examples of artifacts:

tools   weapons   dishes

Artifacts help us learn how people lived in the past.

Things we use today could become artifacts studied in the future!

Complete the table:
- Write P by the artifacts from the <u>past</u>.
- Write T by the items people use <u>today</u>.

Items Used in Daily Life

to get food	shopping cart		bow and arrow	
to write messages	quill and ink		computer	
to travel	car		horse and carriage	
to listen to music	gramophone		mp3 player	

Jamestown

In 1606, about 100 colonists sailed from England to present-day Virginia. Their journey took five long months!

The colonists chose a spot along a river as their new home. They named their new settlement **Jamestown**.

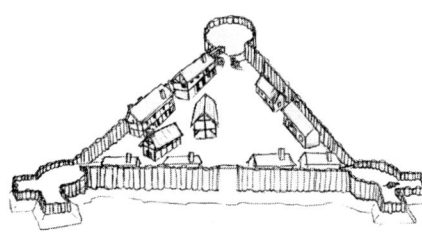

The colonists knew they needed a safe home. They built a wooden fort with wood from trees. The fort was shaped like a triangle. Each corner had a raised area for cannons.

American Indians lived in the area. The chief was named **Powhatan**. He had a daughter named **Pocahontas**.

The Jamestown settlers used their physical surroundings to live. Match each resource with how the settlers used it.

river

build buildings and forts

trees

grow crops

land

bathe, drink, and catch fish

Pocahontas

Pocahontas went with her father's people to visit the settlers at Jamestown. She was very curious about the settlers. She helped the settlers get food from the Indians. She sometimes brought messages from her father.

Pocahontas helped Jamestown's leader Captain John Smith when he was captured by the Indians. He said they laid him on the ground. He thought he would be killed! Pocahontas put her head over his body to save his life!

Circle pictures of food that Pocahontas may have brought to the settlers.

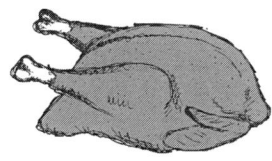  

GEORGE WASHINGTON

George Washington was born in Virginia. At that time, America was a new country!

George grew up on his father's tobacco farm. His father died when George was 11. George helped his mother take care of the farm.

In his early twenties, George joined the Virginia militia. He fought in the French and Indian War. After the war, George got married. He owned a lot of land in Virginia. He built a house. His home was called Mount Vernon. George Washington was an important person in Virginia!

Look at the photograph of Mount Vernon. Read the sentence. Circle the correct answer to fill in the blank.

Mount Vernon was built _____.

recently   long ago

Mount Vernon

Number the events of George's life in chronological order from 1 to 3.

George gets married.	George joins the militia.	George is born.
_____	_____	_____

First U.S. President

When the American Revolution began, George Washington was named commander of the American army. He was a very smart general. George led the fight for freedom from England!

Once the war was over, George Washington was elected the first **president of the United States**. He received every single vote!

George Washington was a leader. He helped establish a new country. He helped design the American government we still live under today!

> George Washington is known as the "Father of Our Country."

Circle the words that describe George Washington.

leader   American   English

president   general   brave

Circle the correct word to complete each sentence.

1. George Washington was born in _____.

    England   Virginia   Washington, D.C.

2. George Washington was a _____ in the American Revolution.

    cook   teacher   general

3. George Washington was the first _____ of the United States.

    president   senator   teacher

Thomas Jefferson

Thomas Jefferson was born in Virginia. He grew up on a large farm.

Thomas went to college. He became a lawyer. He served in the local government in Virginia.

When the 13 colonies wanted to become a free nation, Thomas got involved. He went to meetings to talk about independence.

independence: freedom from the control or influence of another

Thomas was an excellent writer. He wrote the **Declaration of Independence** for the new nation.

The Declaration of Independence was adopted on July 4, 1776. That day is America's birthday!

Do you know the difference between a fact and an opinion?
A fact is a statement that can be proven.
An opinion is someone's feelings that cannot be proven.
Read each statement. Write F for a fact and O for an opinion.

_____ 1. Thomas Jefferson was born in Virginia.

_____ 2. Thomas Jefferson was the best writer in the colonies.

_____ 3. Thomas Jefferson wrote the Declaration of Independence.

THIRD U.S. PRESIDENT

Thomas Jefferson continued to serve the American people after the United States was formed. He held many positions in government, including:
- Governor of Virginia
- U.S. Minister to France
- U.S. Secretary of State
- U.S. Vice President

In 1800, Thomas Jefferson was elected president of the United States! He was the third U.S. president. While president, he lived in the White House in Washington, D.C. Thomas Jefferson was a great leader who helped develop a new country!

**A president's term lasts for four years.
Thomas Jefferson was president for two terms.
How long was Thomas Jefferson president?**

Color the White House. _____ years

Thomas Jefferson appears on the two-dollar bill and the nickel!

Abraham Lincoln

Abraham Lincoln was born in a log cabin in Kentucky. When he was seven years old, his family moved to Indiana. Abraham worked on the family farm.

Abraham was very tall and strong. He taught himself to read, write, and do math. He especially loved to read. Abraham held many jobs. They included a woodcutter, boat driver, store clerk, and postmaster.

Abraham was elected to the Illinois state government when he was 25 years old. He decided to study law and became a lawyer.

People liked Abraham Lincoln. He was admired for his honesty. People called him "Honest Abe."

Circle the picture that shows one of Abraham Lincoln's jobs.

Circle the word that means the same as "honest."

angry   lying   truthful

16th U.S. President

In 1860, Abraham Lincoln was elected the 16th president of the United States. Not long after he was elected, southern states left the Union. They decided to form their own country. Abraham Lincoln believed the country must stay together. Soon, the Civil War started between the northern states and the southern states.

The Civil War lasted for four years until the Union finally won. President Lincoln wanted to reunite the states peacefully. But he was shot and killed just a few days after the war ended. Americans were shocked and sad!

Abraham Lincoln was one of America's greatest presidents. He was a strong leader during a very hard time in American history. He helped keep the United States together!

Circle the correct word or phrase to complete each sentence.

1. Abraham Lincoln was born in _____.

    Ohio   **Illinois**   **Kentucky**

2. Abraham Lincoln really liked to _____.

    cook   **read**   **ride horses**

3. Abraham Lincoln was president during which war?

    Civil War   **World War II**   **American Revolution**

George Washington Carver

George Washington Carver was born in Missouri. He was the son of slaves. George often got sick as a child. He was not strong enough to work in the fields so he worked in the house and the yard.

George left home when he was 10 years old to attend a one-room school. He was very curious. He wanted to learn!

George was interested in science and plants. He went to a college that specialized in farming. It was a big accomplishment for George to graduate from college. Very few African Americans finished college at that time!

How are you like George Washington Carver when he was young? How are you different?

Circle the picture of who might say each sentence. You can circle both pictures sometimes.

1. "I go to school."   George as a boy   Student Today

2. "My school has one room."   George as a boy   Student Today

3. "I like to play video games."   George as a boy   Student Today

4. "I like to spend time outside."   George as a boy   Student Today

Great Scientist

George Washington Carver got a job at the Tuskegee Institute in Alabama. The soil in Alabama was worn out from cotton and tobacco crops. The farmers needed help!

George discovered that new crops would help make the soil healthy again. Two of these crops were peanuts and sweet potatoes. George started experimenting with those crops. He invented hundreds of products that could be made from them.

George Washington Carver became well known as a great scientist! He received many awards during his life.

**Draw a circle around new crops that George worked with.
Draw a square around old crops they replaced.**

**Farmers in the South had worn out the soil.
Put a ✓ by George's solution to that problem.**

☐ 1. bring in new soil

☐ 2. water the soil more

☐ 3. grow different crops

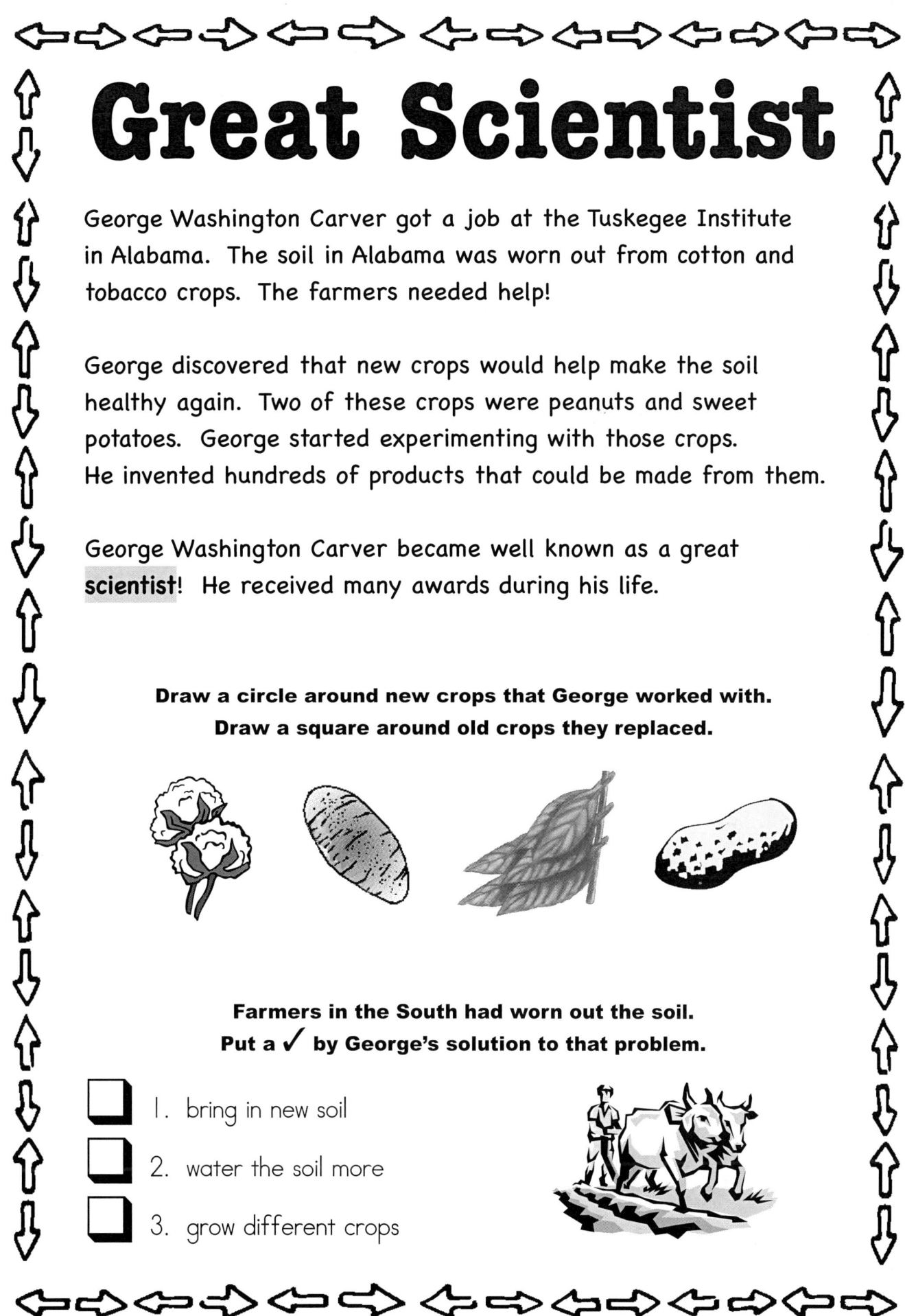

Martin Luther King Jr.

Martin Luther King Jr. was born in Georgia. His father was a pastor at a church. Martin was an excellent student. He entered college when he was only 15 years old! He decided to become a pastor like his father.

Martin grew up in the South. At that time in the South, African American people did not have the same rights as white people did. Martin and many others thought that was unfair. Martin wanted to change things!

Martin urged people to protest in ways where no one would get hurt. He organized nonviolent protests like marches, prayer vigils, and sit-ins. A "sit-in" was a protest where people would sit in a place (like a restaurant) and refuse to leave.

Circle the word that describes the rights of African Americans when Martin Luther King Jr. was young.

fair   unfair   equal

Circle the picture that shows a nonviolent protest.

Civil Rights Leader

Martin Luther King Jr. became a leader in the Civil Rights Movement. That was the time in America when African Americans worked hard to gain equal rights!

In 1963, Martin Luther King led a peaceful protest in Washington, D.C. It was called the "March on Washington." People came from all over the country. The March on Washington was a success! Soon, the U.S. government passed laws to make sure African Americans would have equal rights.

Martin Luther King Jr. is one of America's greatest leaders! Every year, Americans remember him on the Martin Luther King Jr. Day holiday in January.

Number the events 1, 2, 3 in the order they occurred.

_____ 1.   Martin Luther King Jr. led the March on Washington.

_____ 2.   Martin Luther King Jr. was born in Georgia.

_____ 3.   Martin Luther King Jr. became a pastor.

There are hundreds of streets in America named after Martin Luther King Jr.

What Maps Show

A map is a drawing that shows what places look like from above. Most maps show things smaller than they really are!

- A map can show an area as small as your neighborhood. A map can show an area as big as the United States, or the world!

- A map of your town may include streets, lakes, railroad tracks, and important buildings like schools and churches.

- A map of the United States may show states, highways, rivers, and mountain ranges. A map of the world may show continents, oceans, and countries.

Look at this neighborhood map and answer the questions.

1. What street is Country Inn located on?

   _____

2. What business is located at #9 Broad Street?

   _____

3. If you are hungry after a trip to the library, what food is sold next door?

   _____

4. What street crosses the railroad tracks? _____

Globes Are Great!

A **globe** is a round model of Earth.

Globes show large landforms and bodies of water.
Like maps, globes help us see where places are located.
Like maps, globes help us learn what places are like.

**Find the United States on the globe.
Trace the outline of the United States in red.**

What color is water on the globe? What color is land on the globe?

_____   _____

Shapes of Places

Maps show the shapes of places. You can find things on a map by looking at their shapes. All the states have unique shapes. Individual states and the United States can be found by their shapes on maps and globes.

This map shows the shape of the United States of America. Trace the United States in blue.

Find your state in the United States. Color your state red. Color the rest of the United States yellow.

Where Are We?

You can use a map or globe to locate where you live.

You live on the continent of North America.

You live in the country called the United States of America.

Find the United States. Color the United States blue. Be sure to color Hawaii and Alaska—they are part of the United States.

Map of North America

Maps Can Show Land

A **landform** is a shape or feature of Earth's surface. Landforms include mountains, valleys, and more. Maps show where landforms are located.

Landforms affect where people build houses and communities.

Examples of landforms:

mountain	**hill**	**valley**	**coastal plain**	**island**
area of land, usually with steep sides that rise high above the land around it	rounded area of land higher than the land around it, but not as high as a mountain	low land between mountains or hills	flat, low area near the ocean	area of land surrounded by water

Identify each landform shown.

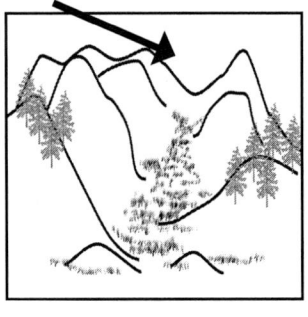  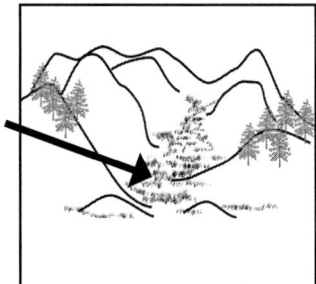

1. _____ 2. _____ 3. _____

 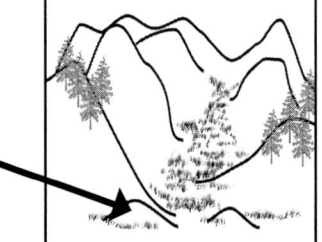

4. _____ 5. _____

MAPS CAN SHOW WATER

Bodies of water are water features of Earth's surface. Bodies of water include oceans, lakes, rivers, and more. Maps show where bodies of water are located.

Water affects where people build houses and communities.

Examples of bodies of water:

lake	**pond**	**river**	**creek**	**ocean**
large body of water surrounded by land	small body of water surrounded by land	large, natural stream of water that flows over land	small, natural stream of water that flows over land	large body of salt water that covers nearly three-fourths of Earth's surface

Identify each body of water shown.

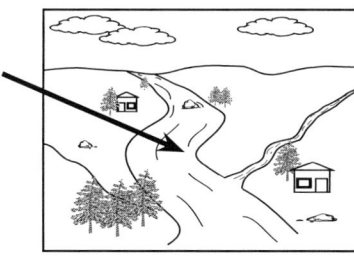
1. _____

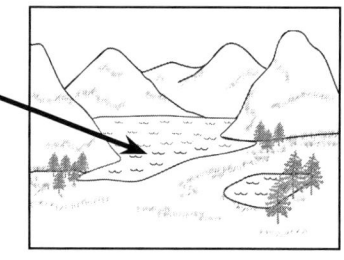
2. _____

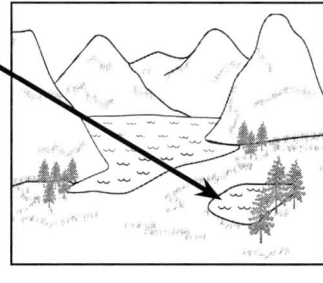
3. _____

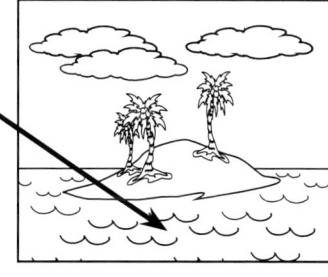
4. _____

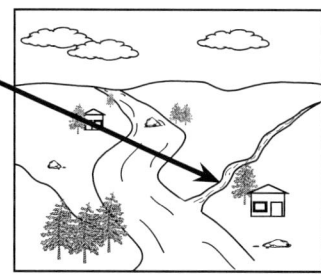
5. _____

Map Titles

A **map title** tells the name of a map or what kind of map it is.

A map title is a useful tool. Different maps show different places. The map title helps us know what we are looking at!

Circle the map title on each map.

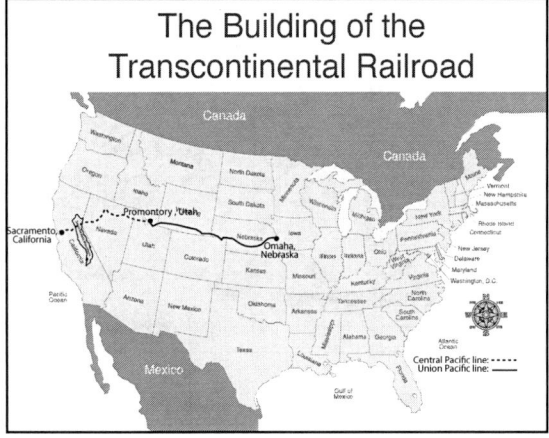

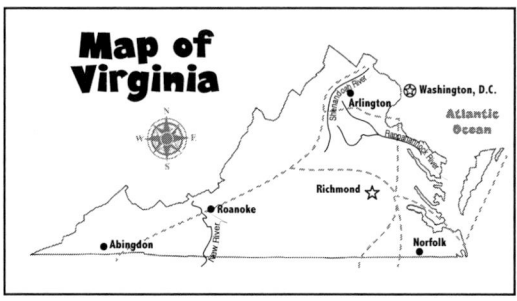

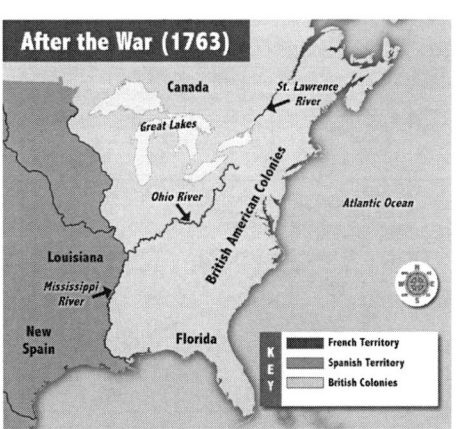

MAP SYMBOLS

A symbol is a picture or thing that stands for something else. Map symbols show us where things are located. Map symbols help us find land, water, cities, roads, and other features.

Draw a copy of each map symbol.

FEATURE	SYMBOL	COPY
Road	⌒	
City	●	
Capital	☆	
River	≈≈	
Coal	COAL	

Make up your own symbols for these.

FEATURE	MY SYMBOL
Farm	
Fort	
Railroad	
Mountain	
Cows	

A **map legend** explains what each shape or symbol used on a map stands for.

A map legend can also be called a **map key**.

These are map symbols.

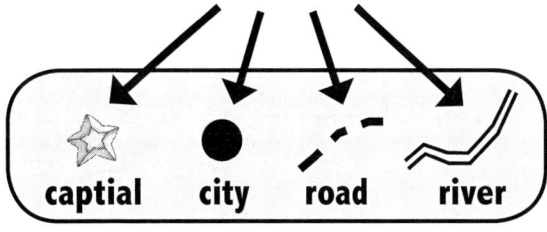

This is a map legend.

Cardinal Directions

Cardinal directions are these directions:

> north   south   east   west

A **compass rose** is a symbol that shows cardinal directions on a map.

Label the compass rose with cardinal directions:
- **Write N for north in the box on the top of the compass rose.**
- **Write S for south in the box on the bottom of the compass rose.**
- **Write E for east in the box on the right of the compass rose.**
- **Write W for west in the box on the left of the compass rose.**

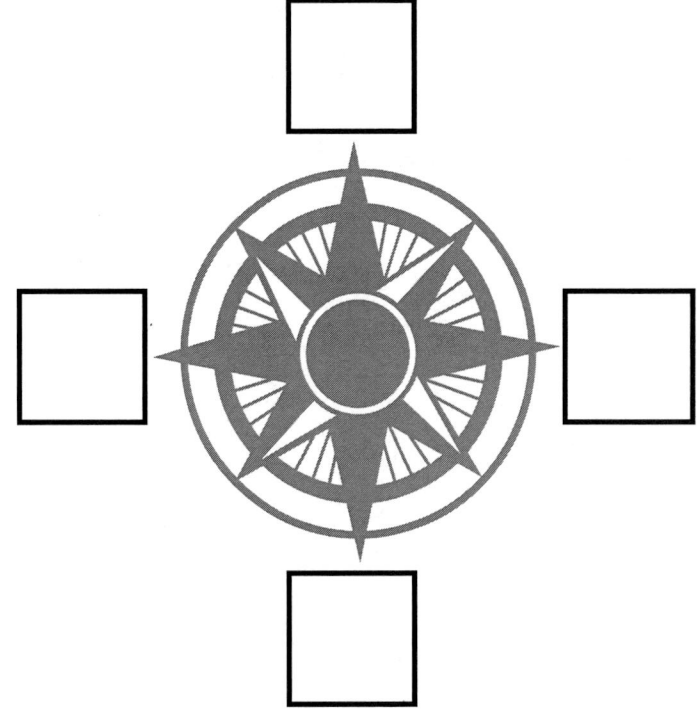

Use a Compass Rose

A **compass rose** shows cardinal directions on a map.
Cardinal directions can help describe where places are located.
You can use cardinal directions to find places on a map.
They can help you find places on Earth!

Use the compass rose to find the locations and answer the questions.

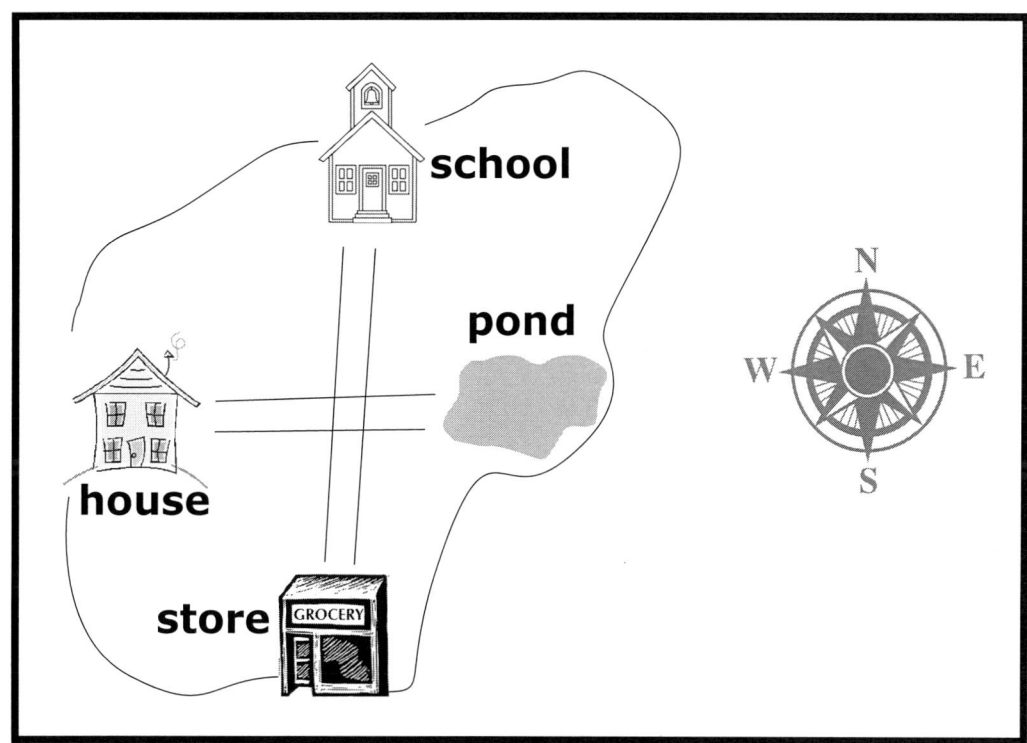

1. Circle the building north of the grocery store in red.
2. Circle the place east of the house in blue.
3. What direction would you travel to go from the pond to the house?

    north　　　**south**　　　**east**　　　**west**

4. What direction would you travel to go from the school to the grocery store?

    north　　　**south**　　　**east**　　　**west**

Make Your Own Map!

Maps can show familiar places like your neighborhood, classroom, or playground.

1. Draw a map of your classroom below.
2. Make your map legend.
3. Label your compass rose to show North, South, East, and West. Good Luck!

MAP LEGEND

CONTINENTS

A **continent** is a large body of land on Earth.
Earth has seven continents.

Find each continent on the map.
- Color North America blue.
- Color South America red.
- Color Australia orange.
- Color Antarctica brown.
- Color Asia green.
- Color Europe yellow.
- Color Africa purple.

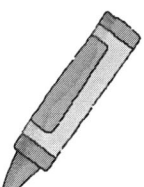

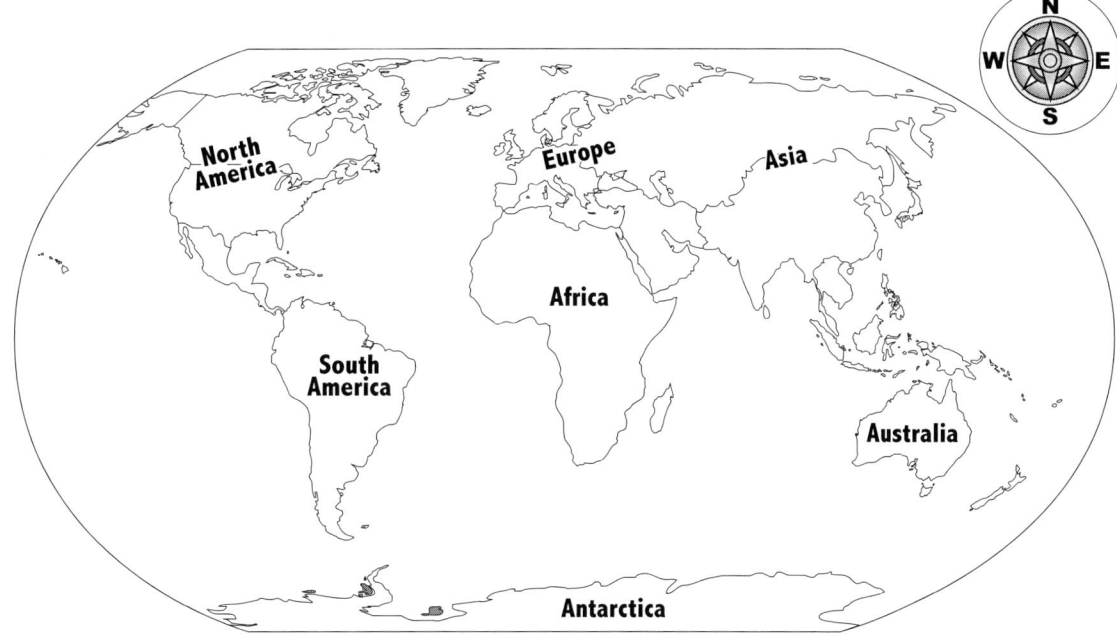

You live on the continent of North America.

Circle North America on the map above.

OCEANS

An **ocean** is a large body of water on Earth.
Earth has five oceans:

      Arctic   Atlantic   Pacific
          Indian   Southern

Find each ocean on the map. Underline each ocean name.
- Write A on the Atlantic Ocean.
- Write P on the Pacific Ocean.
- Write I on the Indian Ocean.
- Write AR on the Arctic Ocean.
- Write S on the Southern Ocean.

Color the continents green.

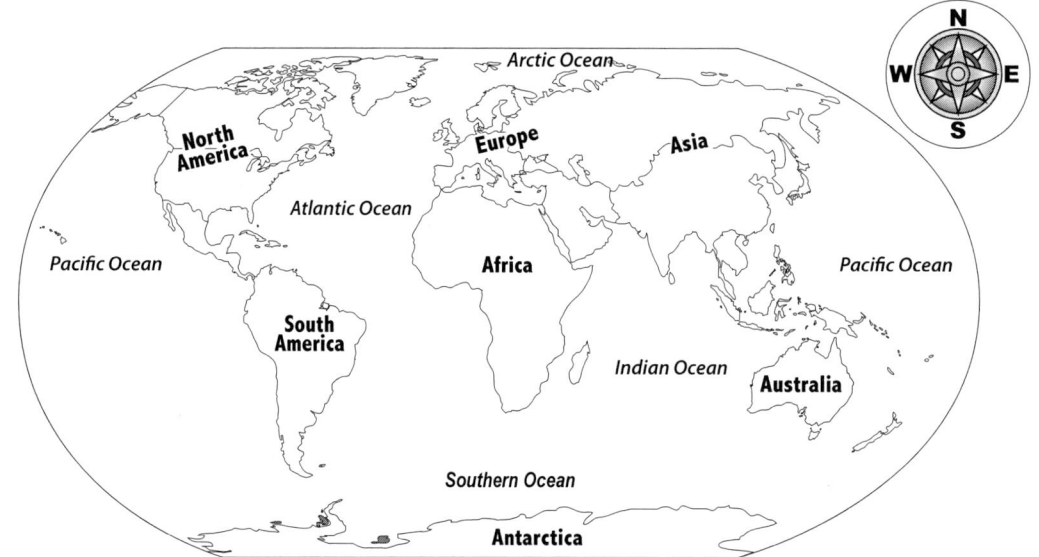

Circle the correct answer to complete each sentence.

1. An ocean is a large body of _____.

      land   water   people

2. Earth has _____ oceans.

      7   5   2

Our Nation's Capital!

The United States has a **capital city**.
The capital of the United States is Washington, D.C.

The president and other American leaders make important decisions here. The White House and Congress are located in Washington, D.C.

The symbol for the capital of the United States is a star inside of a circle.

Draw a star inside of a circle on Washington, D.C., the capital of the United States.

State Capitals

Each state in the U.S. has a **capital**. The capital is the city where leaders meet and make important decisions for the state.

Capitals can be found on maps by looking at symbols. The capital of each state is marked with a star.

Find your state capital and circle it!

Do you know the name of your capital city? Write it here:

_____

What is Geography?

Geography is the study of location, climate, and physical surroundings.

- **Location** is where a place is on Earth.
- **Climate** is the kind of weather an area has over a long period of time.
- **Physical surroundings** are land and bodies of water in a given location.

Location, climate, and physical surroundings affect the way people in a community meet their needs and wants.

Write L under the picture that shows location.
Write C under the picture that shows climate.
Write PS under the picture that shows physical surroundings.

Seasons Change!

A **season** is any one of the four phases of the year.
The four seasons are spring, summer, fall, and winter.

Weather changes each season.
Seasons determine what the weather is like in an area.

Color the pictures of the four seasons.

Match the pictures with the season you would use them in.

| WINTER | SUMMER |

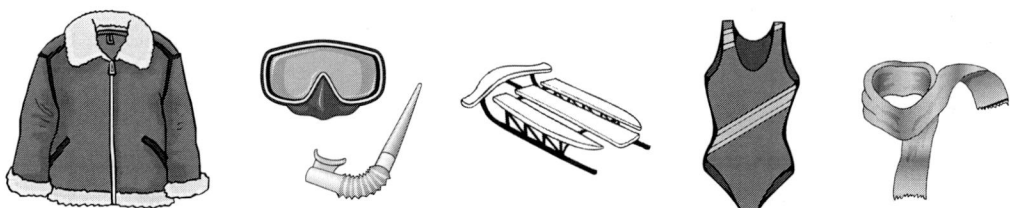

Unique Features

Every place is unique based on its physical and human features.

- **Physical features** are natural parts of the land.
  Examples: lakes, rivers, hills, mountains, and forests
- **Human features** are things that people have added to a place.
  Examples: a city, farm, park, playground, house, or even a traffic light

Circle the features your community has.

mountain   lighthouse   ocean   church   park

lake   river

Think about your community. Compare the land near your school to the land near your house or apartment.

Circle the features that are found on the land near your school in blue.
Circle the features that are found on the land near your home in red.

houses   hill   playground   trees   signal

Which features are found near both places? _____

_____

The Environment

The **physical environment** is the natural world around you.

Early settlers used their physical environment to survive! Their food, clothing, and shelters depended on their physical environment. For example:
- They planted crops that grew well in their climate.
- They hunted animals that lived nearby.
- They made clothing from animal skins.
- They built shelters from trees and plants in the area.

Circle the pictures that show things early settlers depended on the environment for.

Geography Impacts Meeting Needs

The location, climate, and physical surroundings affect the way people meet their needs and wants today. This includes the foods they eat, clothing they wear, and types of houses they build.

Circle the things your community has.

mountain   lake   bear   ocean   river   cow   snow

People in different areas meet their needs in different ways.

> People who live near mountains get lots of snow. They might live in warm cabins with fireplaces. They can hunt deer for food.

> People who live near the beach get sun and warm weather. They might live in cool houses with air conditioning. They can catch fish for food.

Write M by what people use in the <u>mountains</u>.
Write B by what people use near the <u>beach</u>.

Physical Surroundings Affect Jobs

Where people live affects the work they do. Some locations are better than other locations for certain types of work.

Here are some examples:

People who live on open land with rich soil might have jobs growing crops.

People who live near the ocean might have jobs building ships.

People who live in a desert climate would not have jobs fishing!

Match each job to the correct picture to identify the type of work people in each environment might do.

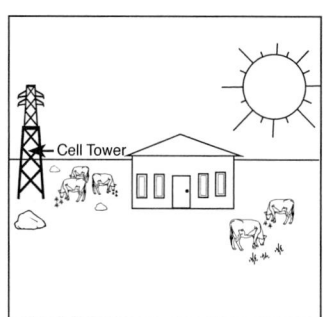

1. _____
2. _____
3. _____
4. _____
5. _____
6. _____

JOBS

a. farmer
b. lumberjack
c. fisherman
d. cell tower repair
e. ship builder
f. raising cattle

Goods Are Good

Goods are things people make or use. You can see and touch goods. Goods include clothes, food, cars, toys, houses, and furniture.

Circle the pictures that show goods.

Circle the good in each sentence.

1. My mom bought a new car.
2. My sister bought some lipstick.
3. I bought a cookie at the store.
4. My friend got a new bike for his birthday.
5. My teacher gave me a pencil.
6. I have new shoes.

Services Are Special

Services are activities people do for other people. Services include haircuts, music lesson, and car repairs.

Write S under the pictures that show services.

_____   _____   _____   _____   _____

People provide services in your community.

Draw a line to match each picture of a service to the benefit that service provides.

Keeps your school clean

Serves you food

Fixes your car

Drives you to school

Producers and Consumers

A **producer** is a person who makes goods or provides services. Examples of producers are:
- cooks: provide food to hungry people
- doctors: provide healthcare to people who are sick
- teachers: provide lessons to students in school

A **consumer** is a person who uses goods and services. Consumers use goods and services to meet needs and wants. You are a consumer. Everyone in your family is a consumer too!

Write C in each square that shows a consumer.
Write P in each square that shows a producer.

We Consume and Produce

People can be both **producers** and **consumers**.

When the barber cuts your hair, he is a producer.
When the barber buys his dinner, he is a consumer!

For each photo, write P by the producer and C by the consumer.

**For each set of photos:
Write P next to the picture of the producer.
Write C next to the picture of the consumer.**

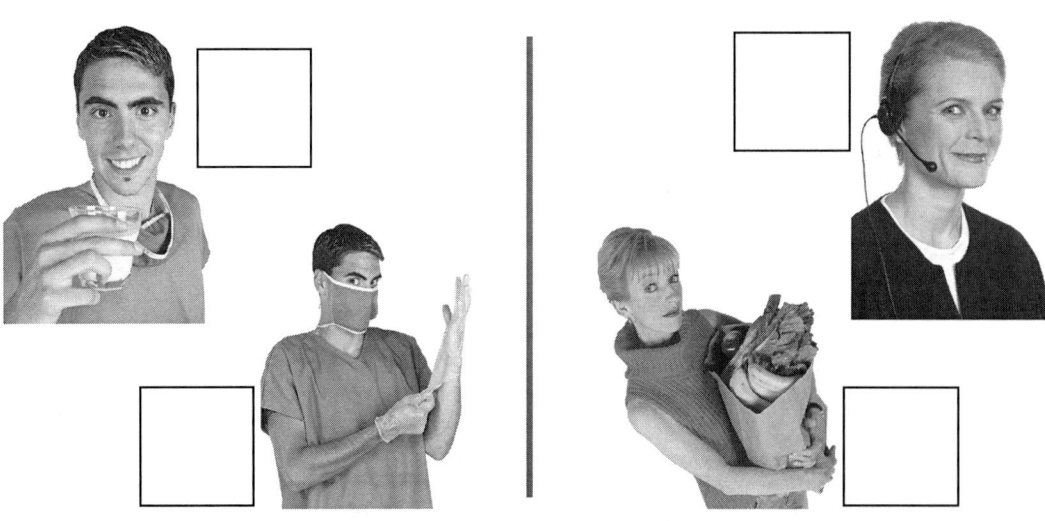

Scarcity

People want many goods and services. Our wants are **unlimited**.

Resources are things that can be used to meet our wants. A resource can be money, people, equipment, or even time. Resources are **limited**. There is a limited supply of them.

We cannot have all the goods and services we want. We have to make choices because of **scarcity**.

 **scarcity:** when unlimited wants are greater than limited resources

Circle the answer to each question.

1. Amara and Scott both want a piece of cake. But there is only one piece of cake left. What is the limited resource?

    ice cream　　　**cake**

2. Jason has $10. He wants to buy a new hat or a new T-shirt. He does not have enough money for both. What is the limited resource?

    money　　　**hat**

3. Adyson made a bracelet. She wants to give it to her mom. She also wants to give it to her best friend. What is the limited resource?

    friends　　　**bracelet**

4. Liz wants to play basketball and soccer. But both teams practice on the same day. What is the limited resource?

    time　　　**basketballs**

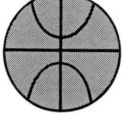 

5. If you were Liz, what would you choose?

Costs and Benefits

People cannot have all the goods and services they want. People must make **choices**. People can choose some things, but they must give up others.

All decisions involve **costs** and **benefits**.

You can make better decisions when you think about the costs and benefits of your possible choices.

> A <u>cost</u> is what you give up when you decide to do something.
>
> A <u>benefit</u> is something that satisfies a want.

Cost/Benefit example:

You have one dollar to spend. You can buy a candy bar or keep the dollar. You decide to buy the candy bar.

Your <u>cost</u> is the dollar. You don't have that dollar anymore, plus you cannot use the dollar to buy anything else.

Your <u>benefit</u> is the candy bar you got to eat! You're not hungry anymore, and it sure did taste good!

**Pretend you got $20 for your birthday.
Think of an idea of how you might like to use the money.
Write your idea. Then list costs and benefits of that choice.**

How I might use my $20: _____

Benefits	Costs

Let's Trade!

People cannot produce every good or service they want. One way people get the goods and services they don't produce is by trading. Trading what you have for what you want is called **barter**.

Early settlers often used barter to get goods and services they did not produce themselves. Farmers and craftsmen could not grow or make everything they needed. They did not always need everything they grew or made. So, they traded! Settlers might trade wheat for cloth or eggs for pottery.

People still barter today. For example, John might fix Bob's computer if Bob will change the oil in John's car.

Circle the correct answers.

1. People _____ produce everything they need or want.

    can   cannot

2. Another word for trade is:

    buy   sell   barter

3. Which person might trade eggs for something they want?

    farmer   doctor   store owner

4. People are consumers when they use barter to buy goods or services.

    true   false

Money!

Money is paper bills and coins. Money is also called **currency**.

Money is used to pay for goods and services. You use money to buy the things you want and need.

How will you pay for it? Match the goods and services with the money you could use to pay for them.

$8.00   50¢ $5.00 $1.45

50¢ $5.00 $1.45 $8.00

Making Choices

Money is a limited resource. We cannot have everything we want.

Sometimes we have to make choices between goods or services we want based on what we can afford. We choose some things and give up others.

Read each story, and put a ✓ next to the best choices.

For her birthday, Bailey's grandmother gave her $20.
Her old book bag was really getting some big holes in it.
Bailey decided to take the money and buy a new book bag.
When she got to the store, she saw a stuffed dog that she really liked.
Now Bailey has to make a choice:

☐ She should buy the book bag.

☐ She should buy the stuffed dog.

Mr. Simmons' car needs new tires. He is afraid they may go flat.
He has enough money to pay for new tires. Mr. Simmons heard on the car radio that his favorite band, White Hot Ice, is giving a concert in his town.
Now Mr. Simmons has to make a choice.

☐ He should use his money to buy a concert ticket instead of tires.

☐ He should get new tires for his car and buy a new White Hot Ice CD if he has enough money.

Now or Later?

People work at **jobs** to earn **money**. People use the money they earn to meet their wants and needs.

People can choose to **spend** money or **save** money.

- When people spend money, they buy goods and services <u>now</u>. But, they give up using that money to buy something they want in the <u>future</u>.

- When people save money, they give up spending <u>now</u> in order to buy goods and services in the <u>future</u>.

Read about Rachel and Evan. Then answer the questions.

Rachel and Evan both get $10 each week for doing chores at home.

Evan likes to play video games. He wants to buy a new game that costs $50, but he doesn't have $50. Every week, he spends his allowance on candy, ice cream, and little toys at the dollar store.

Rachel likes to draw and color. She wants to buy a new art set that costs $50. She decides to save her allowance to buy the art set. After five weeks, she has enough money to buy the art set.

1. Who <u>spent</u> money every week? _____

2. Who <u>saved</u> money every week? _____

3. Who got what they really wanted? _____

4. How did he or she make that happen? _____

Spend or Save?

People can spend money or save money.
People make choices about spending and saving all the time.

When you spend money, you get what you want <u>now</u>.
When you save money, you get what you want in the <u>future</u>.

*People often save money to buy goods and services
that are expensive and that are important to them!*

What is a good or service you would like to buy now?

_____

Can you buy it now or do you need to save for it? Circle your answer.

buy now   save

What is a good or service you would like to buy in the future?

_____

Can you buy it now or do you need to save for it? Circle your answer.

buy now   save

Put a ✓ by ways you like to use money.

☐ Save it in my piggy bank

☐ Spend it on new toys

☐ Spend it on candy

☐ Save it for something big

☐ Save it in the bank

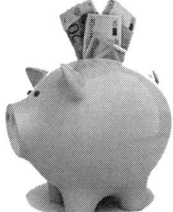

My Community's History

Every local community has a unique history. Communities honor people who helped the community grow over time.

Founder's Day is a day many communities remember people who helped start and grow their community.

Learn about some of the people who contributed to your community over time. As you do, recognize them by adding their names to the street sign and building on this page.

CUSTOMS AND CELEBRATIONS!

American families and communities share **culture**.
We share many of the same **customs**, such as:

- We all celebrate national holidays.
- We all honor national symbols.

We also have celebrations and customs that vary.
Our differences are part of America's **diversity**!

**Circle pictures that show what people celebrate
as a family in green.
Circle pictures that show what people celebrate
as a community in red.**

Good grades

A birthday

Chinese New Year

Memorial Day

Independence Day

A new baby

CULTURE CHANGES

Culture changes over time. New inventions and technology often change culture.

For example, many early Americans spent much of their time farming. When the tractor was invented, farmers could do more work faster. Fewer farmers were needed to grow food for Americans. Many people moved off farms to find towns and cities. The culture was changing!

Inventions like airplanes, computers, and cell phones have changed culture, too. Today, people, products, and ideas travel faster than ever before! Many new ideas spread that way, and culture changes!

Read each sentence. Write T for True. Write F for False.

_____ 1. A country's culture never changes.

_____ 2. New inventions can cause culture to change.

_____ 3. People, products, and ideas travel slower today than in the past.

Circle inventions that have changed our culture.

   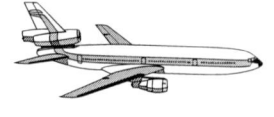

PART OF MANY GROUPS

Characteristics are traits or features. We all have a unique mix of characteristics. But, other people may have some of the same characteristics as we do. We can be grouped with other people who have the same characteristics. We can be part of more than one group!

Complete the steps and answer the questions.

1. Write B by everyone who is a boy.
   How many people are in this group? _____
2. Write D by everyone who has dark hair.
   How many people are in this group? _____
3. Write T by everyone who is tall.
   How many people are in this group? _____

A Diverse America!

America is made up of people with many different ethnic origins. People with different ethnic origins come from many different places around the world.

When people with different ethnic origins came to America, they brought their customs and traditions with them. As they interacted with other Americans, they shared their cultures. Their unique customs and traditions became part of American culture, too!

> An ethnic origin is the place or group of people you come from.
> A custom is something people do as a usual practice.
> A tradition is a custom or belief that is practiced over a long period of time.

Match each ethnic group with the food they brought to America.

____ 1. Italian   A. bratwurst, sauerkraut

____ 2. Mexican   B. pizza, spaghetti

____ 3. German   C. eggroll, rice

____ 4. Chinese   D. tacos, burritos

COMMON TRADITIONS!

Even though Americans have different ethnic origins, they are all still Americans! People of different ethnic origins celebrate American holidays and traditions in addition to their own holidays and traditions.

People in the United States are united as Americans by common principles and traditions. For example, we all say the Pledge of Allegiance to the flag. We all celebrate Independence Day. These traditions unite us as Americans!

Circle the pictures that show people celebrating American traditions and holidays.

Draw a square around the pictures that show people celebrating their own ethnic traditions and holidays.

List a holiday all Americans celebrate.

_____

Model Citizens

Citizens are people who live, work, and play in a certain area. One way people can be good citizens is to use good manners. Good citizens are play fairly when they play games and sports. Good citizens take turns, help each other, and share.

One thing that makes a community great is how the people treat each other. This is also true in your classroom!

Circle the pictures that show good citizens.

What do you think? Put a ✓ by your answer.
Showing good manners is a way to show your respect for other people?
____ TRUE   ____ FALSE

Good Citizens

When you work and play with others, how do you act?
When you act as a good citizen, you help everyone around you!

Good citizens show many positive traits:
- Good citizens **help others**.
- Good citizens **treat others with respect**.
- Good citizens **play fair**.
  Playing fair is honest and gives everyone a chance to win.
- Good citizens **show good sportsmanship**.
  They do not complain when they lose or brag when they win.

respect: thinking and acting in a way that shows others you care about their feelings and their well-being

Circle the pictures that show helpfulness, respect, fair play, or sportsmanship.

Follow the Rules

Rules are guidelines for how people should act or behave. Rules are made so that everyone is treated fairly.

Good citizens follow rules.

It is important to follow rules in your home, school, and community.

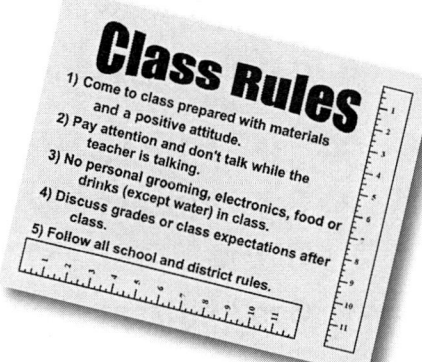

There are good reasons for rules:

- To protect the rights of people
- To keep people safe
- To provide suggestions for good behavior

Match the beginning of each rule with the reason for it.

____ 1. We walk quietly in line down the hall

____ 2. We wait our turn

____ 3. We are quiet when the teacher is talking

____ 4. We obey the crossing guard

A. so that everyone gets a chance.

B. so we don't disrupt other classes.

C. so we don't get hit by a car.

D. so we can hear what she says.

RESPONSIBLE CITIZENS

- Good citizens **take responsibility** for their own actions. That means you are responsible for what you do or do not do. If you have homework and do not do it, whose fault is it?

- Good citizens show **self-control**. They stop themselves from doing what they know is wrong. When you use self-control, you follow the rules.

- Good citizens **value honesty and truthfulness** in themselves and others. Being honest means you tell the truth.

Circle the pictures that show self-control.

What is the honest thing to do?
Circle the correct answers to fill in the blanks.

1. I found some money on the playground. I should _____.

    give it to my teacher   **keep it**

2. I took my sister's cookie when she was not looking. I should ___.

    tell her   **not tell her**

3. I did not finish my homework. I should tell the teacher _____.

    the truth   **I lost it**

Good Citizens Work Hard!

Have you ever heard the story of the grasshopper and the ant?

All summer, the ant gathered food. He knew winter would come and it would be hard to find food. The grasshopper spent the summer playing. He did not plan for the future. When winter came, he had no food. The ant reminded the grasshopper that hard work pays off.

Hard work pays off at school too! If you study hard, you learn a lot and make good grades. Working hard in school will help you when you grow up. One day, your hard work will help you get a good job!

Circle the pictures that show a person working hard.

GOOD CITIZENS VOTE!

A good citizen votes! When you **vote**, you share your opinion about how things should be done. Voting in the classroom is important because it gives everyone an equal chance to make important decisions. Your opinion matters!

One way to participate in decision-making in your classroom is by deciding on class rules. With a partner, look at the two lists of rules below. Each partner should vote by raising his or her hand. Then, circle your vote under each list.

A
Classroom Rules

1. Talk whenever and however loud you want.
2. Don't do your homework.
3. Don't listen.
4. Don't be on time.

My Vote: YES   NO

B
Classroom Rules

1. Do not talk when the teacher is talking.
2. Do your homework.
3. Listen to others.
4. Be on time.

My Vote: YES   NO

Write an idea for a good classroom rule here.

_____

_____

_____

VOLUNTEER!

People contribute to their communities in many ways.
One way people contribute is that they volunteer.

WORD TO KNOW! volunteer: to donate time or effort to a cause without being paid; a person who volunteers

People volunteer to help others.
Places people might volunteer include:

    church   hospital   retirement home   school

          animal shelter   sports team

Circle the correct answer.

People volunteer to make their community a _____ place to live.

      better   worse

Put a ✓ next to things a volunteer might do.

_____ 1. Visit sick people in the hospital

_____ 2. Help the teacher hand out papers

_____ 3. Work as a waiter in a restaurant

_____ 4. Walk dogs at an animal shelter

_____ 5. Clean up trash outside the school

_____ 6. Build houses for the homeless

Vote for Leaders

There are leaders in your city, state, and country.
- The leader of a city is the **mayor**.
- The leader of the state is the **governor**.
- The leader of the nation is the **president**.

People elect leaders by **voting**. These leaders serve the people they represent. They make decisions for the people in the state and local governments.

Match each leader to what he or she might say.

_____ 1. mayor

_____ 2. governor

_____ 3. president

A. "I am proud to be the leader of the United States of America."

B. "I am going to make some changes in this town!"

C. "I will help our state grow!"

Do you know your leaders?

Write the last name of the president of the United States.

_____

Write the last name of your state's governor.

_____

SYMBOLS AND TRADITIONS

The United States has **patriotic** symbols and traditions.
- A **symbol** is a picture or thing that stands for something else.
- A **tradition** is a custom or belief that people do over a long period of time.

Patriotic symbols and traditions honor the people and history of the United States.

patriotic: showing respect and love for your country

**Look at each row of pictures.
Circle the two patriotic symbols that are the same in each section.**

PATRIOTISM

Patriotism is showing love, loyalty, and respect for your country. Americans show patriotism with songs, symbols, and holidays.

Write P next to the pictures that are patriotic symbols of the United States.

Americans sing patriotic songs. The words to these songs show the love and loyalty we have for our country. Americans also say the Pledge of Allegiance. We show respect to the American flag!

Put a ✓ next to the patriotic things we do.

_____ 1. Sing patriotic songs.

_____ 2. Give presents at Christmas.

_____ 3. Say the Pledge of Allegiance.

_____ 4. Never let the flag touch the ground.

"America the Beautiful"

"America the Beautiful" is a famous patriotic song about the beauty of nature found in the United States.

Color the pictures and sing the song!

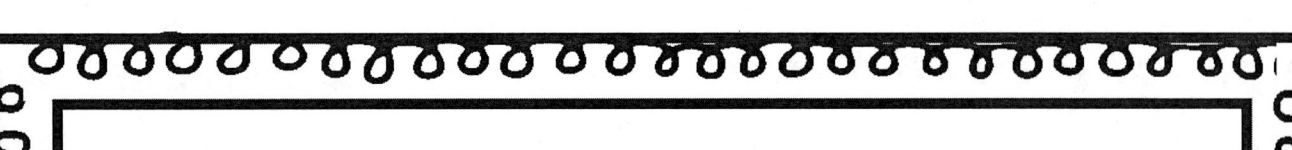

O beautiful for spacious skies,

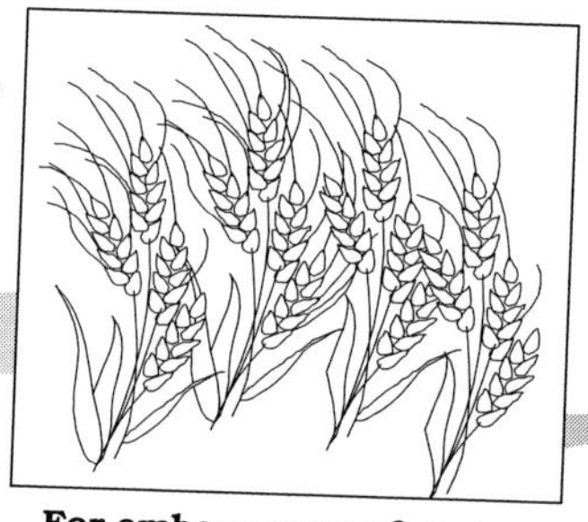

For amber waves of grain,

For purple mountain majesties

Above the fruited plain!

America! America!

God shed his grace on thee

And crown thy good with brotherhood

From sea to shining sea!

"America the Beautiful" was written more than 100 years ago!

"My Country 'Tis of Thee"

"My Country 'Tis of Thee" is a famous patriotic song. It is also called "America."

The words to this song tell how much we love and appreciate our freedom. We don't take our country for granted!

Color the Statue of Liberty.

My country 'tis of thee,
Sweet land of liberty,
Of thee I sing;
Land where my fathers died,
Land of the pilgrim's pride,
From every mountainside,
Let freedom ring!

- In blue, underline the line that tells us America is a land of liberty.
- In red, underline the line that tells that men died fighting for our country.
- In green, underline the line that says America is free!

Circle the main idea of the words to the song.

America has mountains.

America is a free country.

People like to sing about America.

American Flag

The **American flag** is a patriotic symbol of the United States. It represents our country.

Americans often display the flag outside on flagpoles, homes, and buildings.

> When we display and salute the American flag, we show we are proud to be Americans!

Color the flag using the color key.

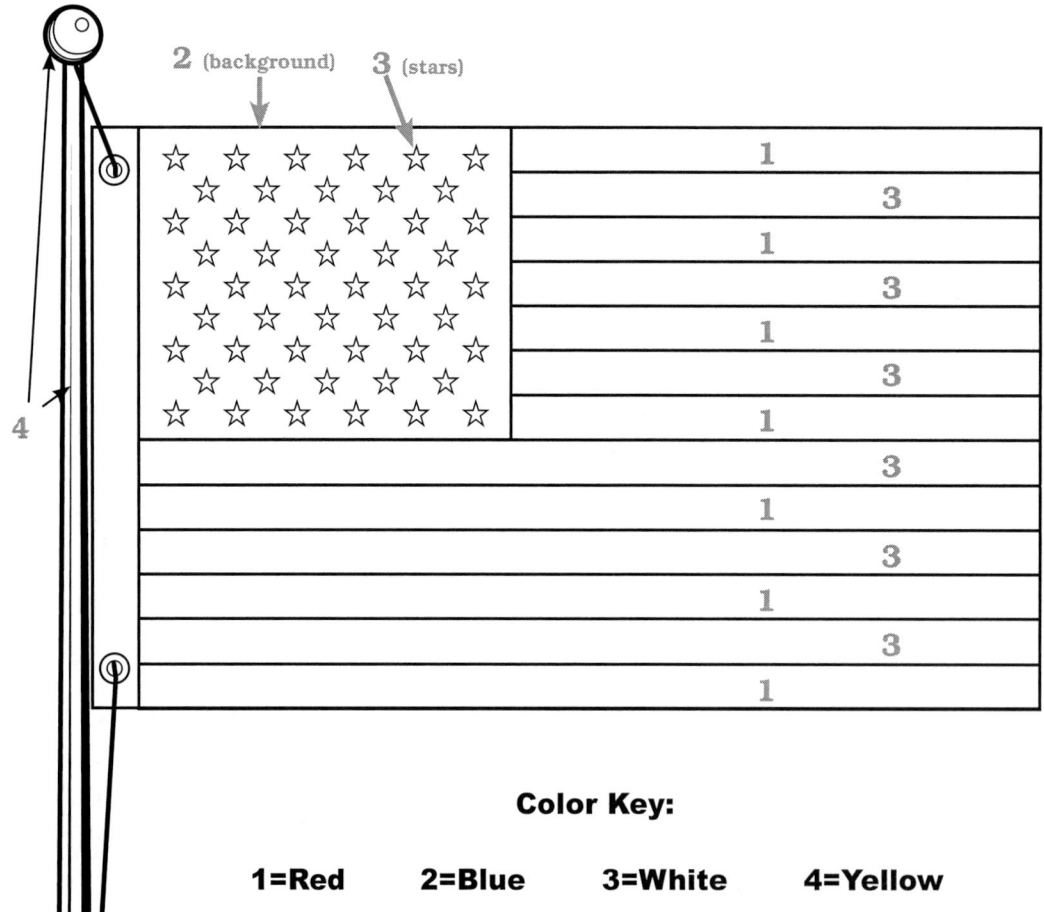

Color Key:

1=Red   2=Blue   3=White   4=Yellow

PLEDGE OF ALLEGIANCE

The **Pledge of Allegiance** is a patriotic <u>tradition</u> that honors the United States.

When we say it, we promise to be loyal to our country and to help keep it great and free.

Color the stars.
Say the Pledge of Allegiance aloud.
Put your right hand on your heart and stand at attention.
Be respectful when you say it.

I pledge allegiance
To the flag
Of the United States of America
And to the republic for which it stands,
One nation under God,
Indivisible,
With liberty and justice for all.

The Statue of Liberty

The **Statue of Liberty** is an American monument. It is located in New York City.

The Statue of Liberty was given to America by France in 1886. It was given as a sign of friendship. Today, the statue is a symbol of freedom for the whole world!

Color the picture of the Statue of Liberty.

What does the Statue of Liberty symbolize? _____

Liberty Bell

The Liberty Bell is an American monument.
It is located in Pennsylvania.
The Liberty Bell has a large crack!

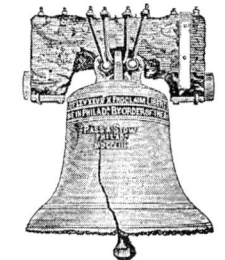

The Liberty Bell was used to gather people for the first public reading of the Declaration of Independence! Today, the Liberty Bell is a symbol of our independence and freedom.

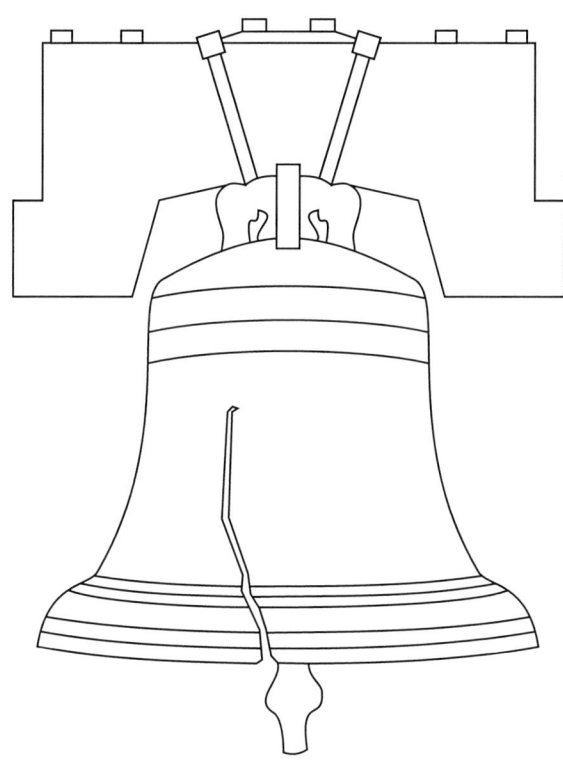

Color the picture of the Liberty Bell.

Write the name of the state where the Liberty Bell is located.

_____

_____

_____

Washington Monument

The **Washington Monument** is a symbol of leadership and independence. It is located in Washington, D.C.

The Washington Monument was built to honor George Washington, America's first president. It is more than 500 feet tall!

Circle the correct answer.

The Washington Monument honors our nation's first president.

TRUE   FALSE

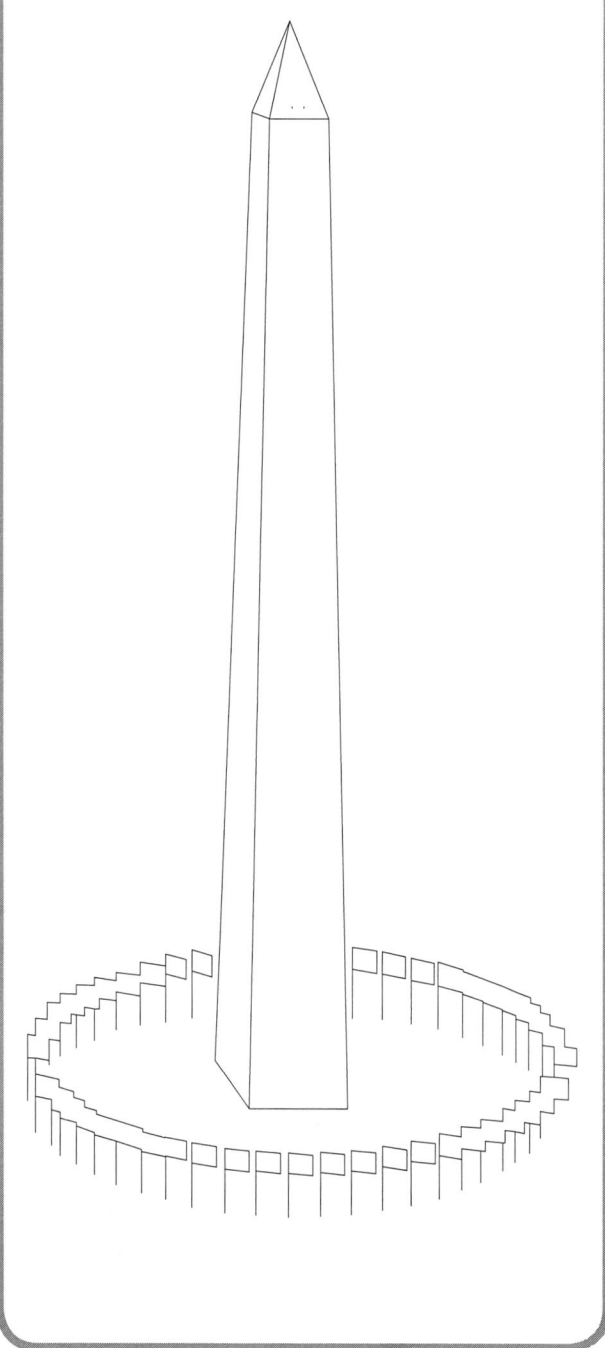

Color the picture of the Washington Monument.

BALD EAGLE

The **bald eagle** is a symbol of the United States.
It stands for power, strength, courage, and freedom.

How many eagles can you find nesting on the mountain?
Circle them.
Write the total here:

_____

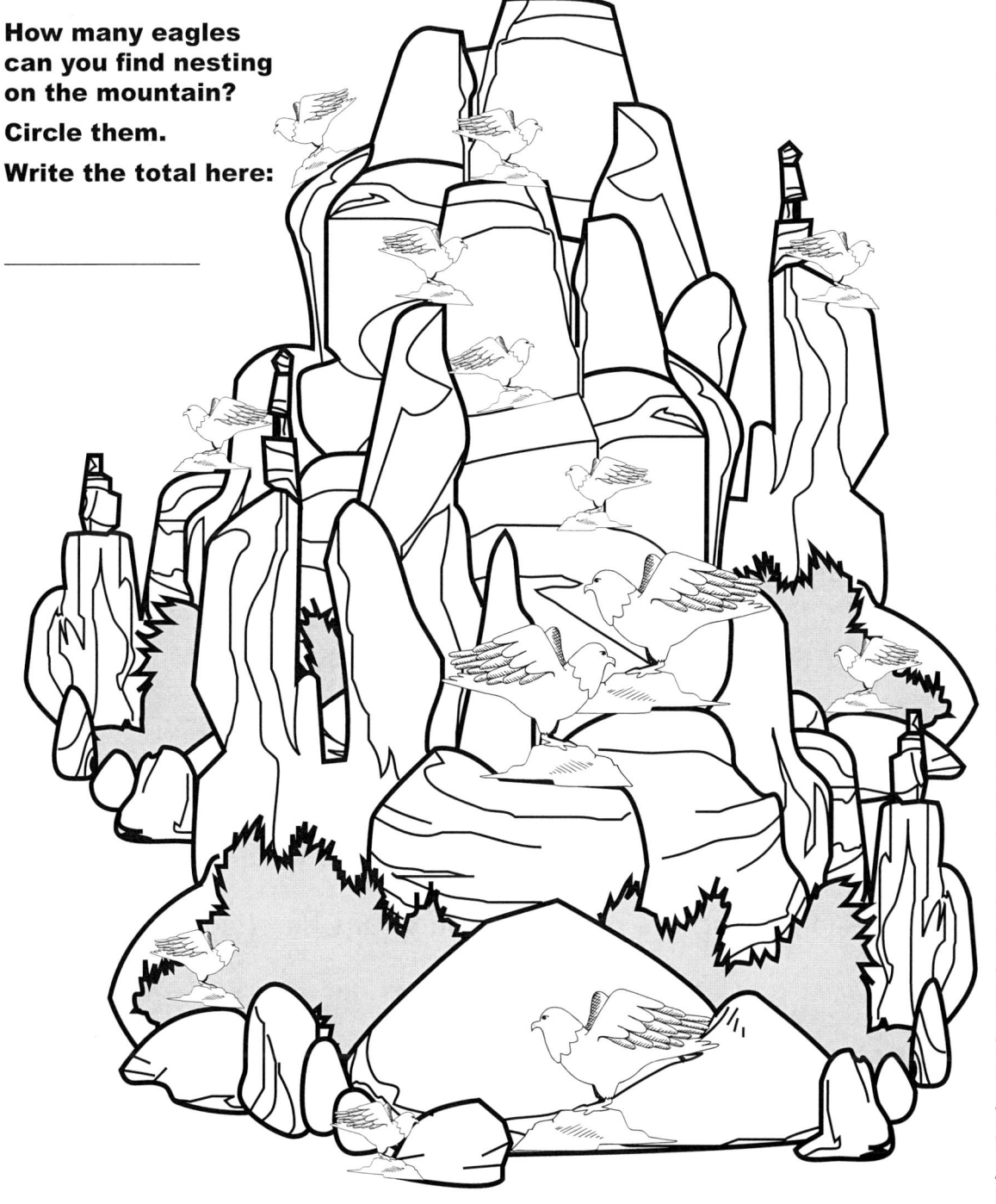

Star-Spangled Banner

The Star-Spangled Banner is our national anthem. This means it is the official song of the United States.

The Star-Spangled Banner was written by Francis Scott Key in 1814.

Someone usually sings the Star-Spangled Banner before many sporting events.

The name of our national anthem is written below with one word missing. Fill in the missing word.

STAR- _ _ _ _ _ _ _ _ BANNER

**Read the words to America's national anthem.
Do you know the tune?**

Star-Spangled Banner

Oh, say can you see by the dawn's early light

What so proudly we hailed at the twilight's last gleaming?

Whose broad stripes and bright stars through the perilous fight,

O'er the ramparts we watched were so gallantly streaming?

And the rocket's red glare, the bombs bursting in air,

Gave proof through the night that our flag was still there.

Oh, say does that star-spangled banner yet wave

O'er the land of the free and the home of the brave?

Independence Day

We celebrate many holidays in the United States! We celebrate holidays to remember important leaders and events of the past.

 holiday: a day on which something or someone is honored or remembered

Independence Day is a holiday to remember when America became a new country.
It is sometimes called America's birthday!
Independence Day is also called the
Fourth of July because we celebrate it on July 4th.

Independence Day is a holiday to celebrate our country's birthday.
Trace the words Independence Day.

Independence Day

Match each picture with a way we celebrate Independence Day.
Use a different color for each line you draw.

Parades

Fly our flags

Fireworks

Sing patriotic songs

Picnics

Sporting events

COLUMBUS DAY

Columbus Day is a holiday to remember Christopher Columbus.

Christopher Columbus was a famous explorer.
He sailed west from Europe. He landed in the Americas.

We celebrate the "discovery" of America by Europeans as Columbus Day. We celebrate Columbus Day in **October**.

Circle the tools that Columbus would have used on his voyage to America.

Presidents' Day

The president of the United States is our country's leader. A special holiday was set aside to honor U.S. presidents. Presidents' Day honors the current president and all presidents from the past.

Presidents' Day is on the third Monday of the month of February each year. February was chosen because two of our most famous presidents, George Washington and Abraham Lincoln, were born in February.

Use the calendar below for this activity.

**George Washington was born on February 22, 1732.
Write GW on George Washington's birthday.**

**Abraham Lincoln was born on February 12, 1809.
Write AL on Abraham Lincoln's birthday.**

Martin Luther King Jr. Day

Dr. Martin Luther King Jr. was an African American. He worked so all people would be treated fairly.

We celebrate **Martin Luther King Jr. Day** in January.

Color the picture of Dr. Martin Luther King Jr.

Trace the word fair.

fair

Draw a picture to show what "fair" means to you.

New Year's Day

New Year's Day is on the first day of the year.
The first day of the year is **January 1**.

On this holiday, Americans say goodbye to last year.
They wave hello to the new year.

Many people set goals for the new year. *Do you?*

Circle the picture that shows New Year's Day.

Write T for sentences that are true.
Write F for sentences that are false.

____ 1. New Year's Day is in February.

____ 2. Many people set goals for the new year.

____ 3. New Year's Day celebrates good times to come.

Veterans Day

On **Veterans Day**, we honor Americans who served in the U.S. **armed forces**. We celebrate Veterans Day in **November**. We fly flags and hold parades.

Thank you, veterans!!!

Color these people in the armed forces.

Memorial Day

On **Memorial Day**, we remember people who fought and died in wars. These veterans made a BIG sacrifice for America. They gave their lives so we could be free.

We celebrate Memorial Day in **May**.

Circle who we honor on Memorial Day.

Decorate the soldier's grave.

LABOR DAY

Labor Day is a holiday to honor Americans who <u>work</u>.

Labor Day is celebrated in **September**.
On Labor Day, people relax from work.
Many people have picnics and cookouts.

Circle who we honor on Labor Day.

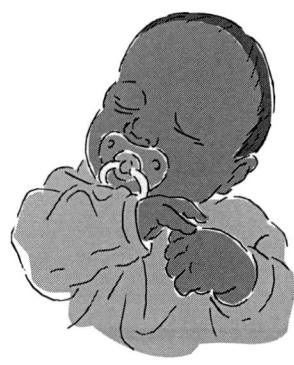

Yearly Traditions

Americans honor the United States through **traditions**. Traditions are things we do every year.

Put a ✓ by each of these traditions you have participated in.

☐ Say the Pledge of Allegiance
☐ Celebrate the Fourth of July (Independence Day)
☐ Celebrate Presidents' Day
☐ Sing the Star-Spangled Banner

Draw a tradition you celebrate on the Fourth of July.

Our President

The United States' leader is called the **president**. The president makes decisions for our country. The president is elected by the citizens of the United States. When you turn 18 years old, you can vote for the president too!

Draw the president at his or her desk. Then color the picture.

Write the president's last name here.

_____

- -

_____

MONTH CALENDAR

This month is:

_____

_____

_____

Sunday	Monday	Tuesday	Wednesday	Thursday	Friday	Saturday

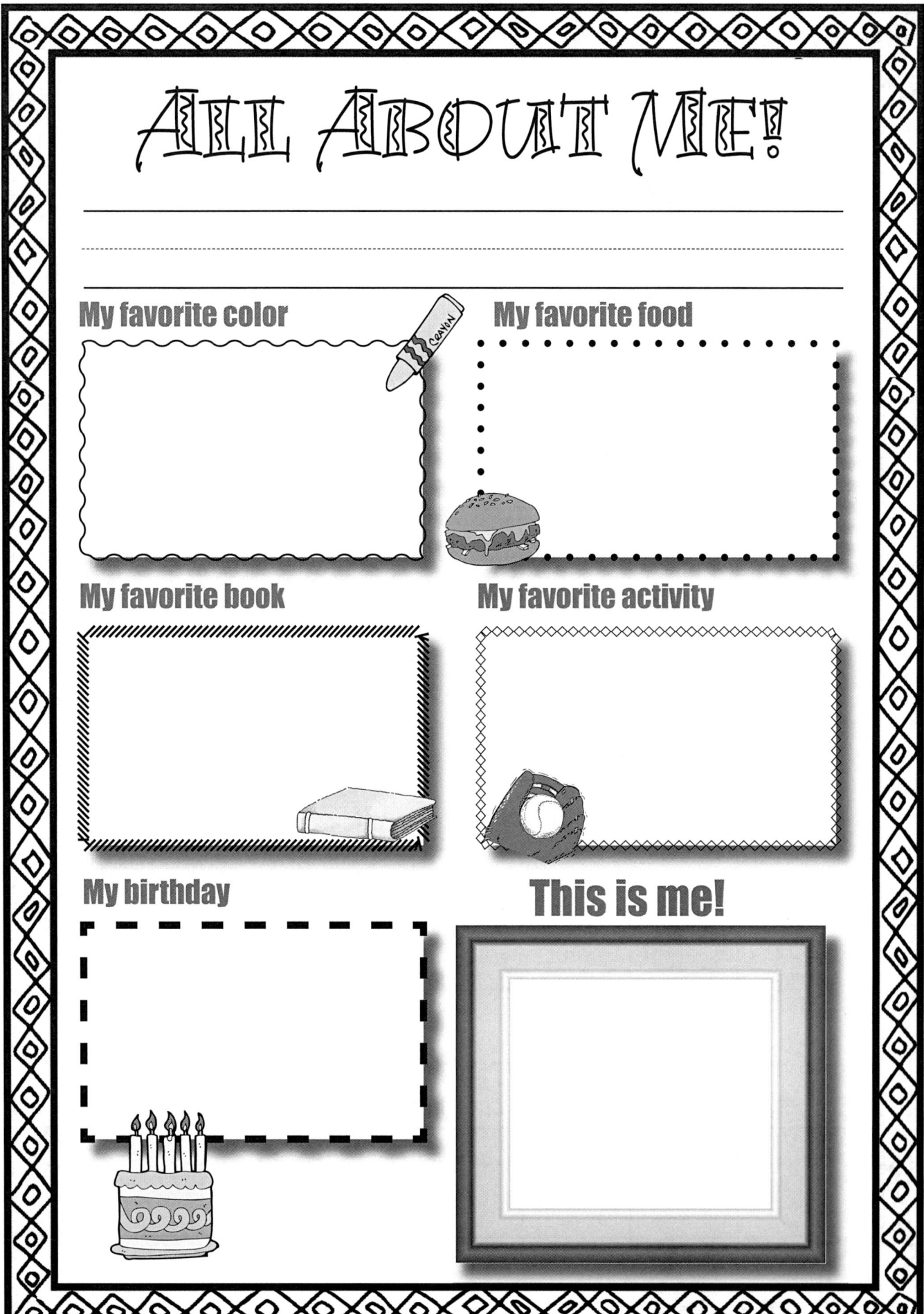

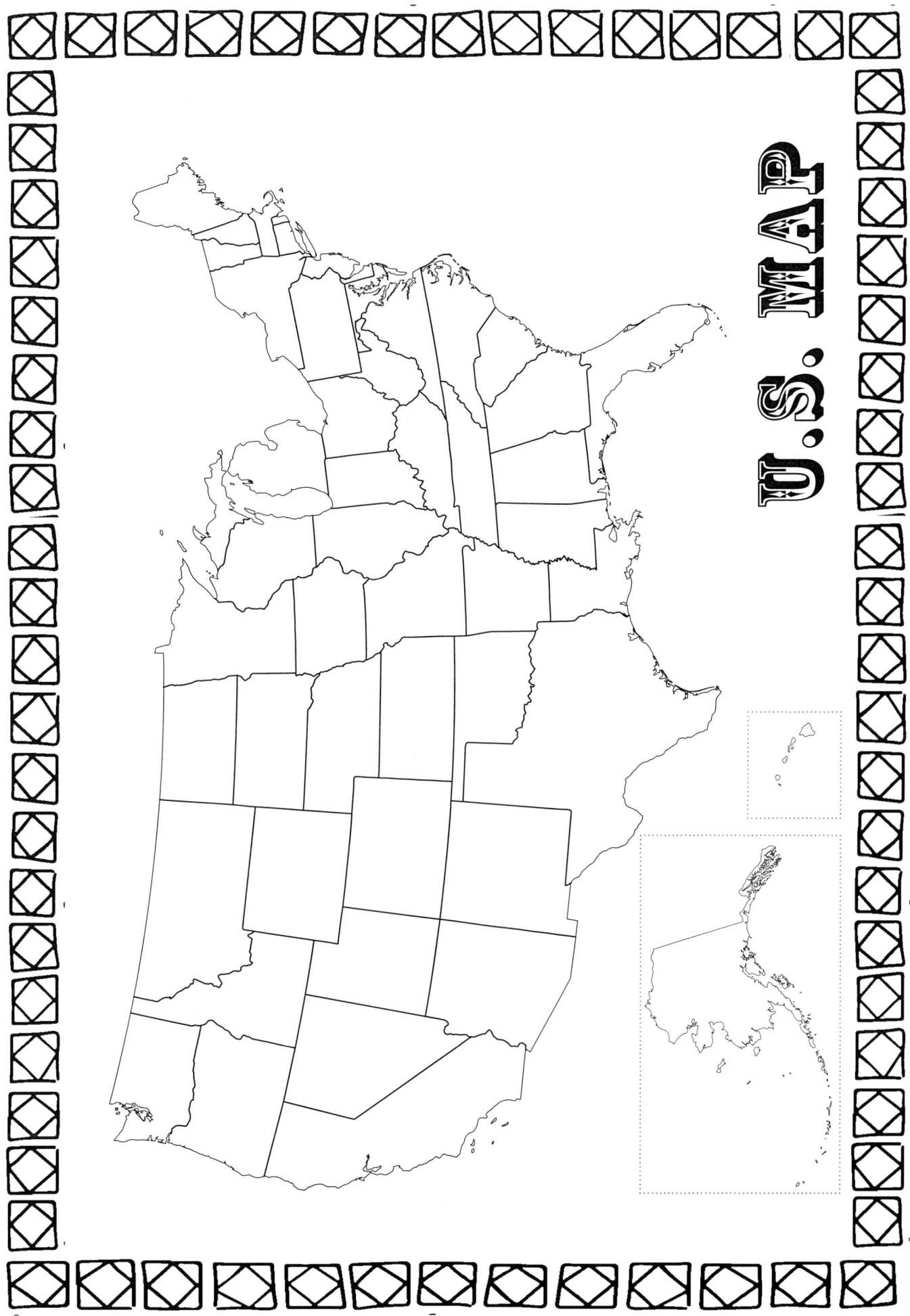

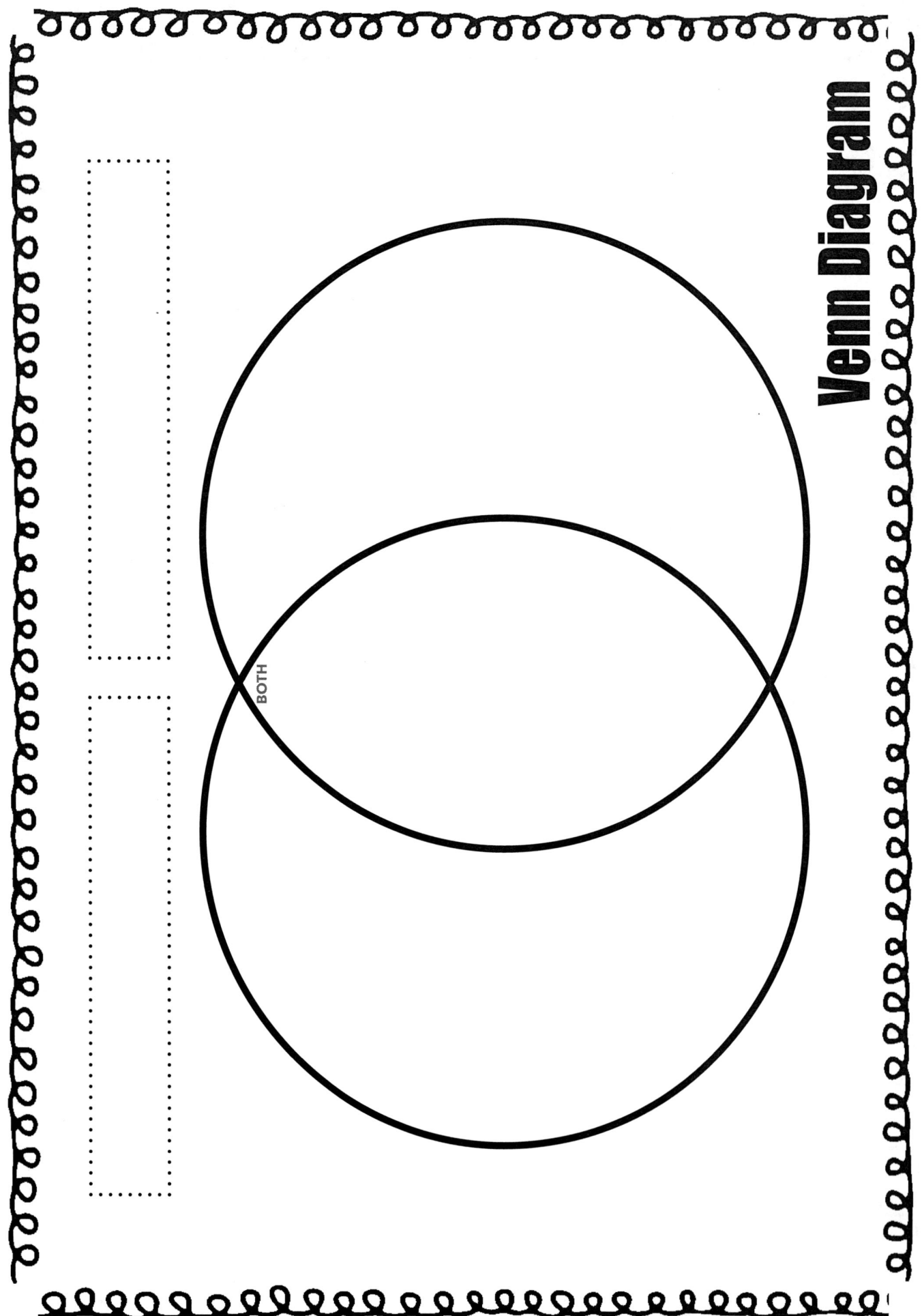

Acrostic Grid

TOPIC:

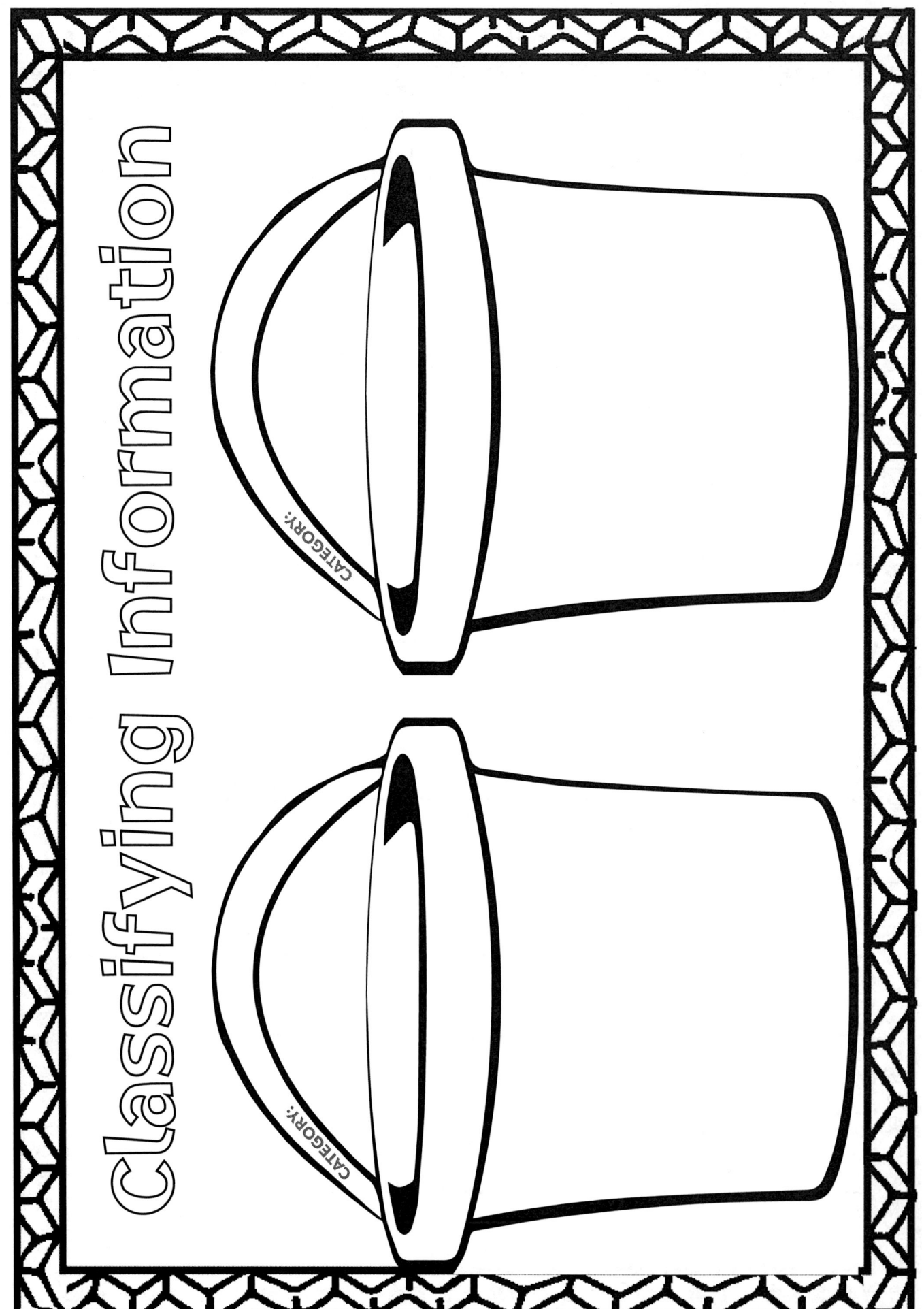

Vocabulary Word Map

Definition	Sentence

Word	Drawing

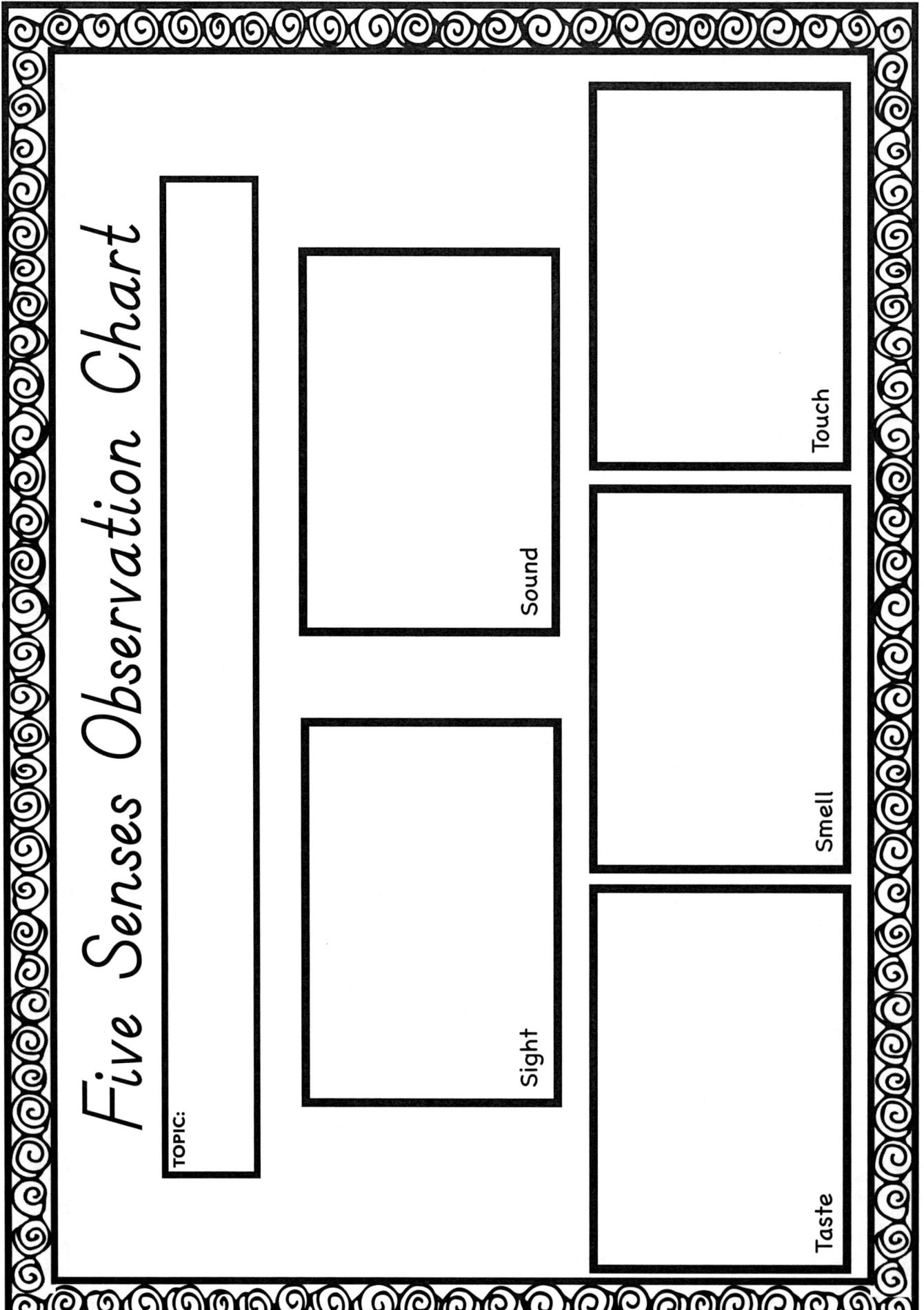

TIMELINE

MY STATE FLAG

Write your state's name:

_____

- -

_____

Draw your state flag.

My State Bird

My state bird is the:

_____

- -

_____

_____

- -

_____

Draw your state bird.

My State Flower

My state flower is the:

_____

_____

_____

_____

Draw your state flower.

MY STATE TREE

My state tree is the:
_____
- -
_____
_____
- -
_____

Draw your state tree.

Writing Prompts

George Washington's Character

From what you have learned about George Washington, choose a character trait you think he possessed. Write several sentences to describe how that character trait helped him become the first president of the United States.

Your Personal Journal

Write a journal entry each day for five days in a row. Use a separate piece of paper for each entry. In your journal entries, describe an event in your life on that day. Think about how you felt about the event. Describe your feelings. Add drawings.

A Page From Pocahontas

Pretend you are Pocahontas. Write a journal entry about a time when you delivered food to the needy settlers at Jamestown. Answer these questions:
- Why did you help the settlers?
- What kind of food did you give?
- How did they react to your gift?
- How did giving food make you feel?

Writing Prompts

COMPARE LEADERS

After you have read the stories about George Washington and Thomas Jefferson, compare the two men in a Venn diagram. Read the stories closely once again to pick out things that are alike about the two men, and things that are different.

Write a Letter to a Famous American

Choose a famous American. What would you like to tell that person? Write a letter to him or her. Explain why you chose to write to them. Thank them for their contributions to American history!

MY FAVORITE SEASON

Write a letter to a friend telling him or her about your favorite season.
- Describe the weather during that season.
- Describe what changes you see outside during that season.
- List things you like to do outside during that season.

Writing Prompts

Sensing The Season

Do you know what the five senses are? They include sight, smell, taste, touch, and hearing. Think of sights, smells, sounds, and things you can taste and touch during the current season. List them in a graphic organizer.

What's Your Environment?

People who live in different environments have different needs. Write a list of needs for people in a cold climate. Write a list of needs for people in a warm climate. Write your lists in a graphic organizer. Compare your answers with those of other students. What different things did you think of?

American Symbol Acrostic

Choose an American symbol like the bald eagle, the Liberty Bell, or the Statue of Liberty. You can just use one word like "eagle," "liberty," or "statue." Write an acrostic poem about that symbol. Decorate the acrostic poem with drawings.

Writing Prompts

Pledge of Allegiance

Read the Pledge of Allegiance. Or, you can or recite it if you have memorized it. Then, rewrite the Pledge of Allegiance in your own words. Decorate your paper with patriotic symbols like stars, flags, and fireworks!

HARD WORK PAYS OFF!

When you work hard and do well at your schoolwork, that will help you later in life! Make a list of five things you can do to succeed in school. After you have created your list, decide which action is the hardest for you to do. Put a #1 by that item. Think about why it is hard for you. Write some ideas of how you can make it easier!

We All Need Goods

Write a journal entry describing a good you or your family has purchased recently. Why did you need that good? Where did you find the good? How did it improve your life or your family's life? Draw a picture of the good on your paper. Or you can find a picture of the good in a magazine and attach it to your paper.

Writing Prompts

WE ALL NEED SERVICES

Think of a service that you or your family has used recently. Write a journal entry describing your experience with that service. Be sure to answer these questions as you write:
- Why did you need the service?
- Where did you find the service?
- How did the service improve your life?
- Would you use that service again?

Saving Money

Write a story about a boy or girl who saved their money to buy something very special. How did the boy or girl get the money to save? How long did it take the boy or girl to save enough to money? What did the boy or girl buy? How did they feel when they bought it?

American Flag Poem

Write a poem about the American flag! Ideas include:
- Describe the flag's colors.
- Describe the stars and stripes on the flag.
- Describe how you feel when you see the flag flying high against the blue sky!

First Day of School—We All Fit Together

This is a way of welcoming your class and letting students know that you will all work together during the school year. (Working together is a common civics theme.) Make a big jigsaw puzzle out of corrugated cardboard with each student's name on a piece of the puzzle. Add a sign above the puzzle that says, "I'm glad you're part of our picture!" Tell each student to find his or her puzzle piece and take it out. Then, help your students reassemble the puzzle one by one as students introduce themselves and insert their personal puzzle pieces.

Vocabulary Flash Cards

Help students make vocabulary flash cards for the words they learn this year. You can provide cards with the word and definition on one side, and have students illustrate each term or concept on the back. Or, you can give students the words on separate cards and let them define and illustrate the words themselves. (Of course, you would need to check the definitions for accuracy.)

Teachers: You can use the Vocabulary Cards included in the book to supplement this activity.

Make a Primary Source Time Capsule

Help your students all contribute to making a class time capsule! For starters, you can take photographs of the class, and students can write letters or journal entries about what they are learning or what they like to do for fun, etc., to include in it. Look for other timely things to add such as a printout of the weekly lunch choices, local newspaper articles, etc. Try to find some items that reflect things that will be different in a year or complete in a year (such as building a new school playground or adding landscaping around the school).

Students can also contribute small token items they will not miss. Explain to students how their time capsule is full of primary sources and artifacts that represent the students and class as of this school year. Once you've collected all the items desired, seal it up, and tell them it will be opened in one year by your next class. If they are the first class to create a time capsule, congratulate them on starting a new tradition. If they are not the first, they will have the fun experience of opening the capsule from the previous year and analyzing the artifacts left by last year's students!

Use Vocabulary Words About Time

Show your class copies of photos, drawings, books, and other artifacts from various historical eras, ranging from many centuries or decades ago to recent history or even today. Ask them to associate each item with the correct chronological vocabulary like "long ago," "recent," "yesterday," "today," etc.

Organize Birthdays in Chronological Order

Conduct an activity that combines months of the year and chronological order. Have each student write down the month and day of his or her birthday on a piece of paper. Mix up the papers, and instruct the class to arrange the papers in chronological order.

Display the papers on a bulletin board in the classroom so students can analyze the results. Which month of the year has the most birthdays in it? Are there any months with no class birthdays?

Historic Person of the Week!

On a bulletin board lined with butcher paper, post the name of a person students are learning about in social studies. Have students add information they learn about that person directly on the bulletin board paper. They can write a fact, add a picture they have drawn or cut out of a magazine, list character traits, create a timeline of life events, etc. At the end of the week, discuss what the class now knows about that person.

Create a Timeline

All students need timeline skills! With help from parents, ask students to create a timeline of their lives on a piece of poster board. Each student should include their birth, when they started to walk, the day they started preschool, and the day they started first grade. Timelines could also include births of siblings, moves to a new house, and any other significant events.

Teachers: If you want to create a simpler timeline, students can use the Timeline template in the book.

Record the Seasons

Post a full-year calendar on the classroom wall. Let students take turns recording basic weather observations and temperatures for each day. Refer to the calendar when discussing how the year is divided into seasons, and include vocabulary about time, months of the year, and seasons.

Make a Newspaper Front Page

Divide your class into groups. Instruct each group to create a newspaper front page on a piece of poster board. Each group should name their newspaper and write it at the top of the poster board. Have each group choose one famous American they have studied during the school year. Then, help them write headlines and short articles about the accomplishments of that famous American on the front page of the newspaper. Students can add drawings or pictures to the page.

Think About Inventions

This is a great inquiry-based learning exercise. Students can set the direction each step of this project takes.

- **Ask students:** What is the purpose of inventions? Write their answers on the board. (Examples might be to solve a problem; to make something better, faster, or last longer; to save people time; etc. Guide students as needed, but be flexible to go with the purposes and wording that they come up with.)

- **Ask students:** Can you give me examples of how inventions have improved life for your family?

- **Ask students:** Do you have any ideas for inventions that could make life easier for you or your family in the future?

- Have students work in small groups to create a drawing, description, or simple prototype of an invention that could do at least one of the things they listed as the purpose for inventions.

- Have a mini-science fair and let students display and discuss their invention ideas.

Map Your Route to School

With their parents' help, ask students to create a map of how they get to school each day. Include their street or neighborhood as the starting point and the school as the ending point. Include major street names, prominent buildings, and features like the neighborhood park or a shopping center. Draw arrows along their route to school. If desired, ask students to include a compass rose and a map legend.

Understanding Human Features

What's around you? Using modeling clay or other art supplies, ask students to draw or create a model of a human feature in your community. It could be a building, a playground, a school, a baseball field, etc. Let students explain what a human feature is, and why the human feature they chose is important to the community.

Observing the World

Give each student a copy of the Five Senses Observation Chart (located in this book). Direct them to bring their chart, a pencil, and a clipboard or notebook (as a hard surface to write on), and go for a walk outside the school.

Have students use their senses to observe the world around them, and then record what they observe on the observation chart.

- What do they see?
- What do they hear (birds, street noise, etc.)?
- What do they smell?
- What features can they touch, and how do they feel (soft, damp grass; hard, rough concrete, etc.)?
- What is the last of the five senses that they will probably not experience on this walk?
- How can they experience the sense of taste at other times?

Back in the classroom, ask students to share their observations. Of course, the observations listed will be varied. Discuss how people can be in the same place but have different experiences!

Project-Based Learning

Kids Can Volunteer Too

Have students model the behavior of good citizens by volunteering to help other students in their class or in the lower grades. Set up a volunteering project where kids can offer ideas to help other people and then sign up to do those things. Ideas for participation in this volunteering project include tutoring, mentoring, reading aloud, or helping to keep orderly and safe behavior in the lunchroom or on the playground.

American Symbols Flash Cards

Create simple flash cards with symbols of the United States, such as Uncle Sam, the flag, the bald eagle, Air Force One, George Washington, the Washington Monument, the Statue of Liberty, etc. Show students the cards, and have them raise their hands to identify the symbol. You might want to list the symbols on the white board and check them off as the students identify them.

Labor Day Game

On individual slips of paper, write down numerous occupations that would be familiar to your students—doctor, teacher, cashier, waitress, nurse, airline pilot, etc. (You may want to write them on the white board to help students with their questions/guesses.)

Place the slips of paper in a basket. Divide your class into groups. One student in each group will pull a slip of paper from the basket. The others in the group will ask several questions to try to determine the job title. For example, "Do you work at a school?" "Do you wear a uniform to work?" "Do you work in a hospital?"

After asking some questions (you can set a time limit), the groups will confer and try to guess the occupation written on the selected slip.

Holiday Collages

Students will learn about many holidays in the early grades. Divide the class into groups and assign a holiday to each group. Give each group a piece of poster board. The first step will be to write the holiday name and month it is celebrated at the top of the board. Then instruct students to cut pictures from magazines that represent that holiday. Have them create collages on poster boards to display around the room.

Thank You Stars on Veterans Day

In the activity, students will make and decorate stars to honor the men and women who have served or are serving in the armed forces.

Collect clean aluminum pie plates and foil pans of all shapes and sizes. Cut the bottom out of the plates/pans. Using a star template, trace and cut out stars from the foil bottoms. Cover the foil edges with colored masking tape to get rid of any sharp edges and make the stars sturdy. Pass out a star to each student. Have them write an adjective on their stars that describes a soldier: brave, strong, proud, patriotic, etc. Students can then decorate their stars with markers, stickers, ribbon, feathers, and other art supplies.

Display the stars on a bulletin board or school hallway around Veterans Day!

Working with Goods and Services

On separate small sheets of paper, have each student draw pictures of three goods they or their family have bought recently. Tell them to write a word or phrase to describe each good.

Next, ask students to draw three services they have used recently on separate small pieces of paper. Tell them to write a word or phrase to describe the service. (The reason for separate sheets of paper is so you can easily redirect any wrongly categorized goods or services to the correct display/bulletin board below.)

Create a "goods" bulletin board or display and a "services" bulletin board or display. Let each student add his or her goods and services to the bulletin boards.

When the displays are complete, issue some challenge questions, such as:

- "How many ____ are on the bulletin board?" (Fill in the blank with an item many students chose, or a broad category such as "pieces of clothing.")
- "Which service was included most often?"
- "Which good do you think costs the most money?"
- "Which goods starts with the letter __?" etc.

Producers and Consumers

Make a chart titled "Producers" and divide it into two columns. At the top of one column, write "People Who Provide Goods," and at the top of the other column, write "People Who Provide Services." Instruct students to name jobs for each side, and add them to the chart. Then have each student choose one job that provides goods or services; ideally different jobs, but you might allow overlap.

Give each student a name tag to wear that lists his or her profession. Have students write "I Produce" on one side of a sheet of paper and "I Consume" on the other.

Students should imagine doing their job and make a list of the goods or services they provide to other people as part of that job on the "I Produce" side. Then they should think of some things they need or want in their daily lives (such as groceries, doctor, car repair, entertainment, etc.) and write them on the "I Consume" side.

Then let students get up and interact with each other, offering what they provide and considering if they would want what the other person provides. Each time they find something else they think they need or want, they should add it to their "I Consume" side, just as other students will hopefully add what they provide to their "I Produce" sides. This is a great way for students to better understand the many different producers that they rely on every day, and see how as a producer, other people will rely on them.

Afterward, ask everyone to raise their hand if they were a producer (all students should); then ask everyone to raise their hand if they were a consumer (all should). Ask students why people are not only consumers but are producers as well. Help them realize that providing goods and services helps them earn income, and that is how they can afford to buy goods and services.

Discuss the interconnected relationship between producers and consumers. What if no one wanted to buy the good or service they provided? (They could produce something people do want to buy instead.) Also explain that many people are producers by providing a service to a company as an employee. Employees provide services like answering phones, driving a truck, cooking in a restaurant, packing and shipping products, etc., that helps a business provide its goods or services. That is how many people earn their income!

VOCABULARY (side 1)

 address

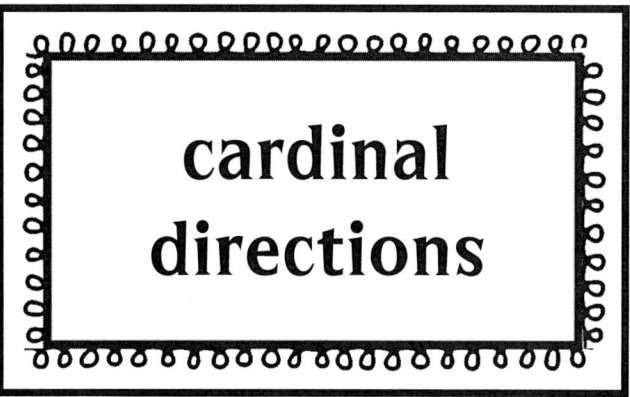 cardinal directions

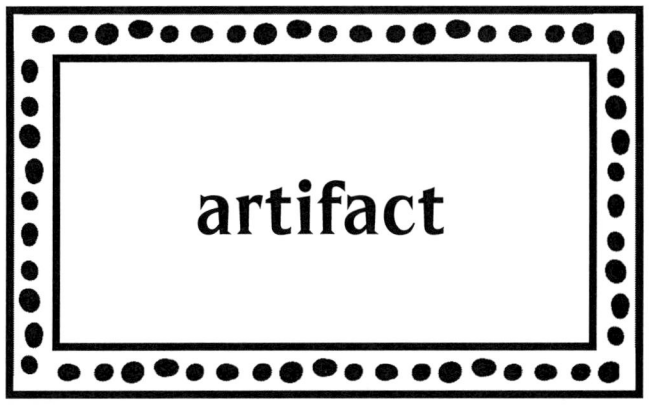 artifact

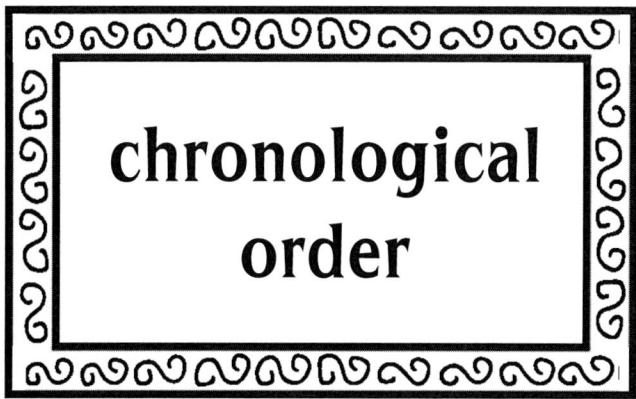 chronological order

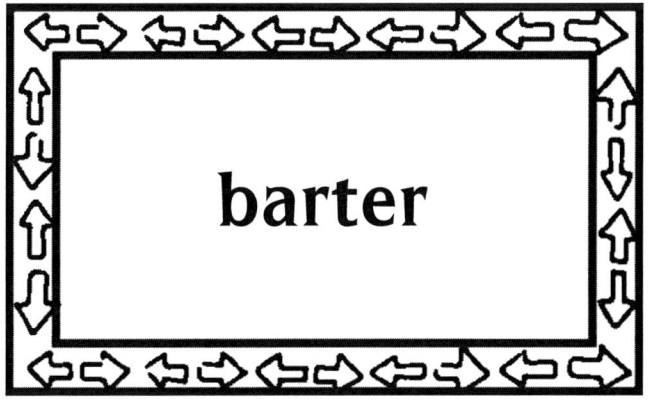 barter

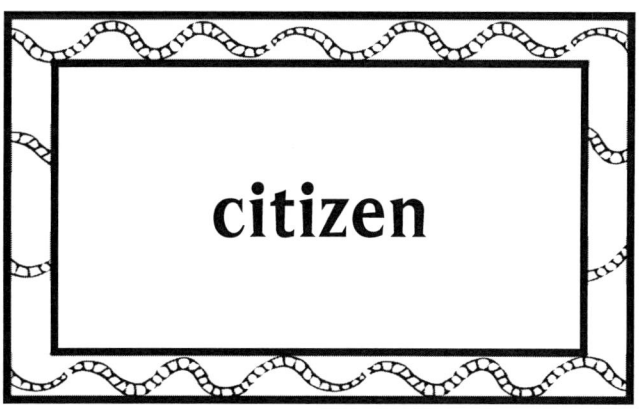 citizen

 calendar

 climate

VOCABULARY (side 2)

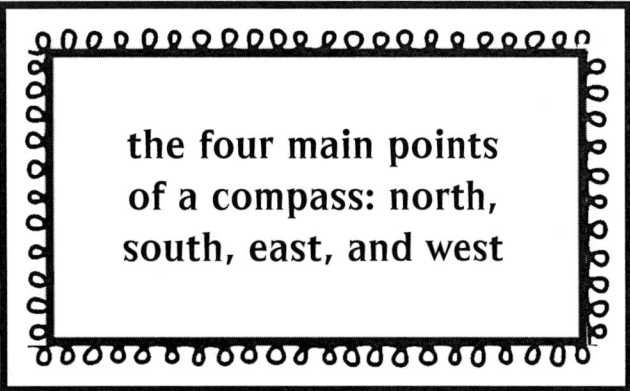

the four main points of a compass: north, south, east, and west

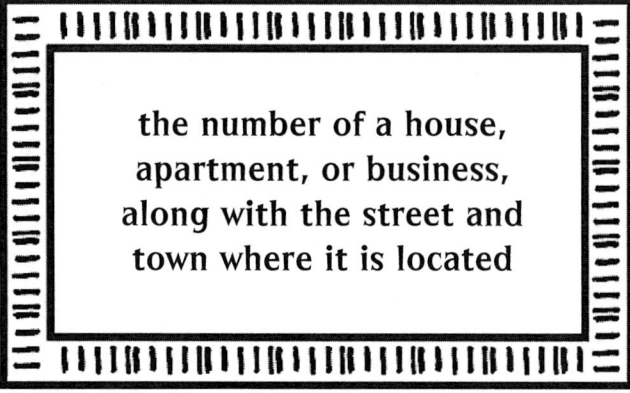

the number of a house, apartment, or business, along with the street and town where it is located

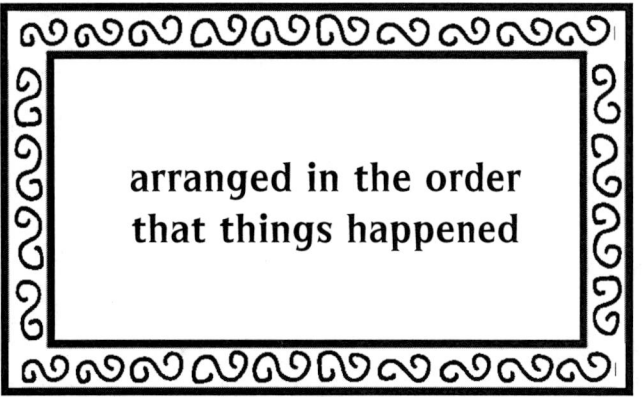

arranged in the order that things happened

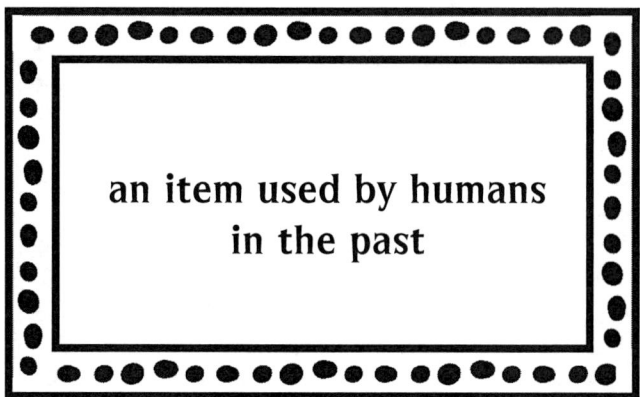

an item used by humans in the past

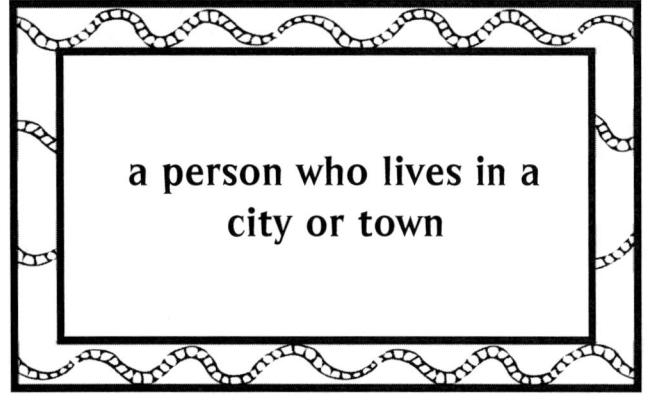

a person who lives in a city or town

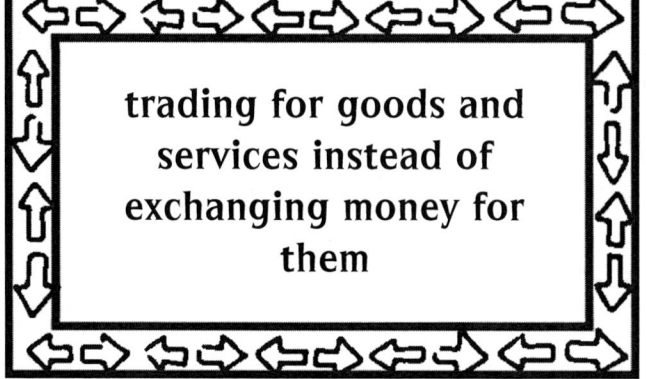

trading for goods and services instead of exchanging money for them

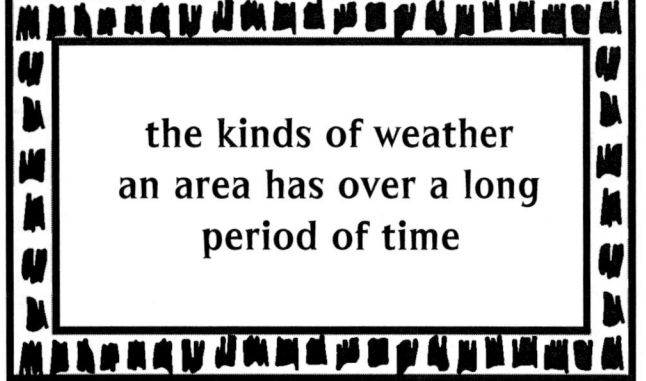

the kinds of weather an area has over a long period of time

a chart or series of pages showing the days, weeks, and months of a particular year

VOCABULARY (side 1)

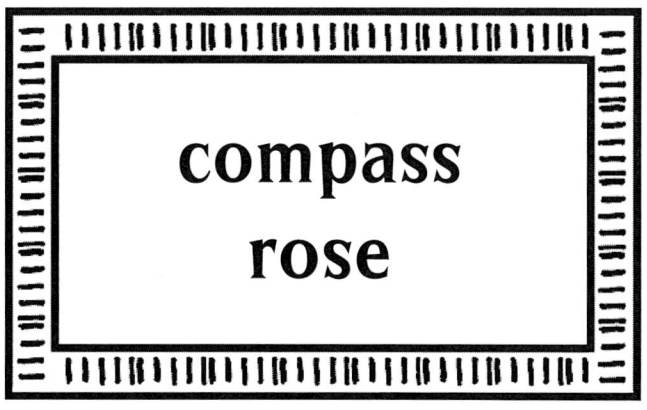
compass rose

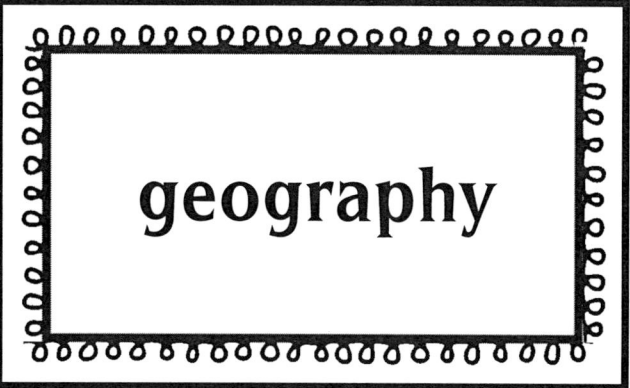
geography

consumer

globe

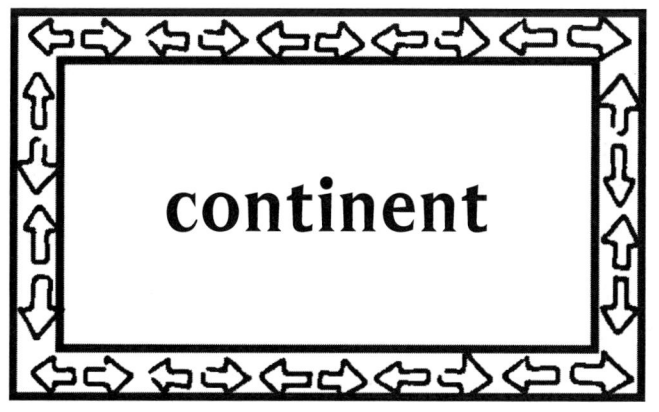
continent

goods

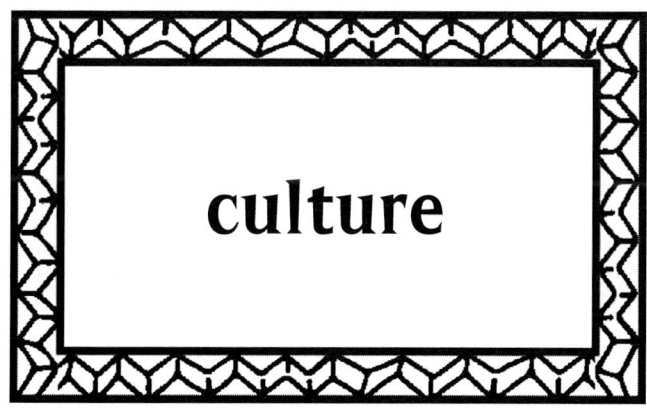
culture

holiday

VOCABULARY (side 2)

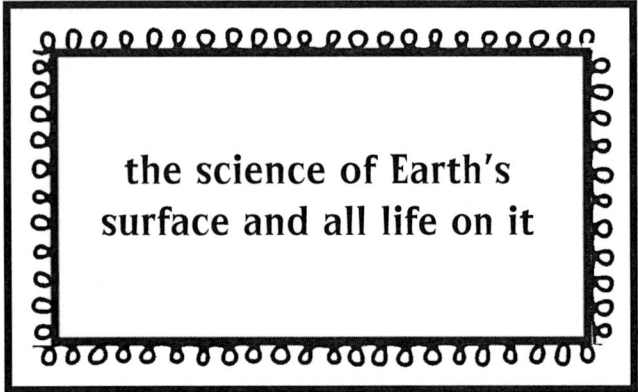
the science of Earth's surface and all life on it

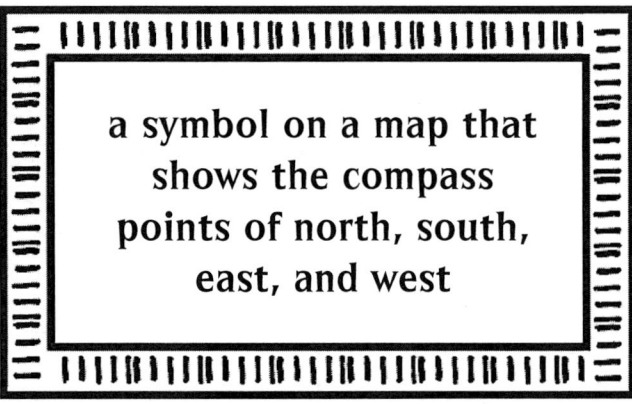
a symbol on a map that shows the compass points of north, south, east, and west

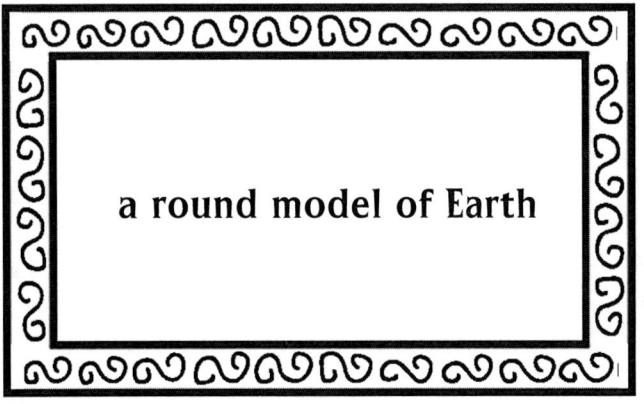
a round model of Earth

someone who uses goods and services

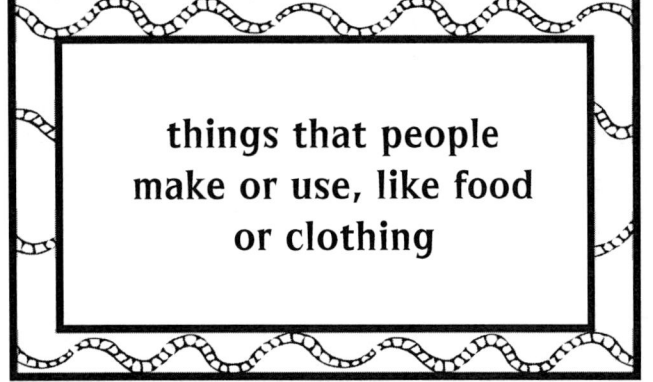
things that people make or use, like food or clothing

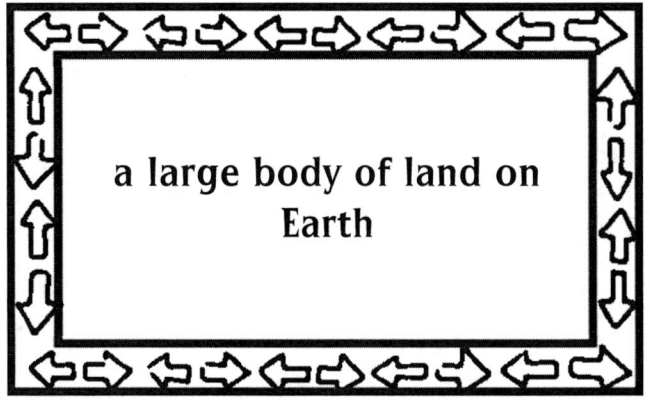
a large body of land on Earth

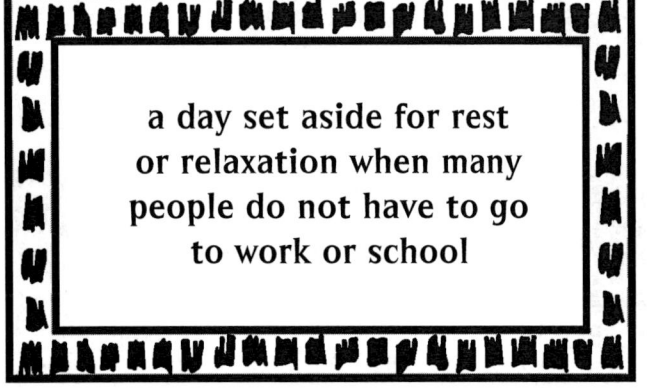
a day set aside for rest or relaxation when many people do not have to go to work or school

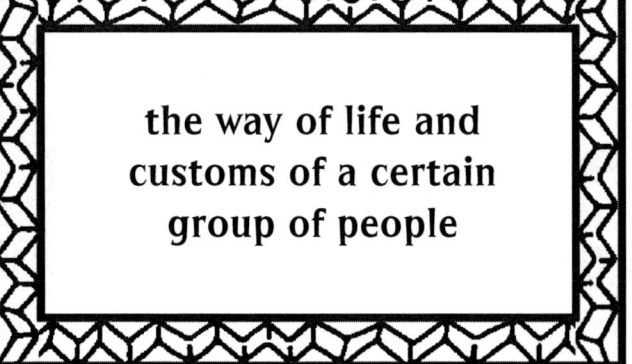
the way of life and customs of a certain group of people

VOCABULARY (side 1)

landform

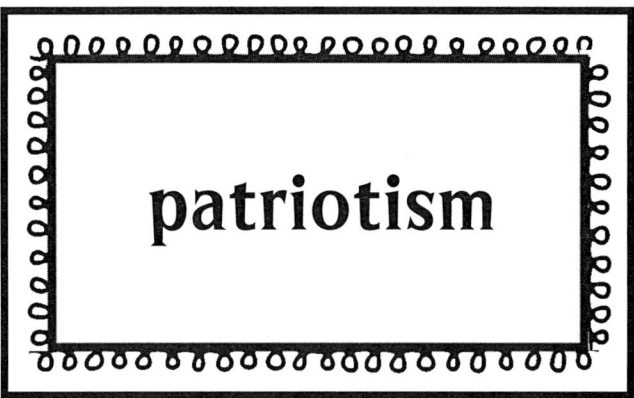
patriotism

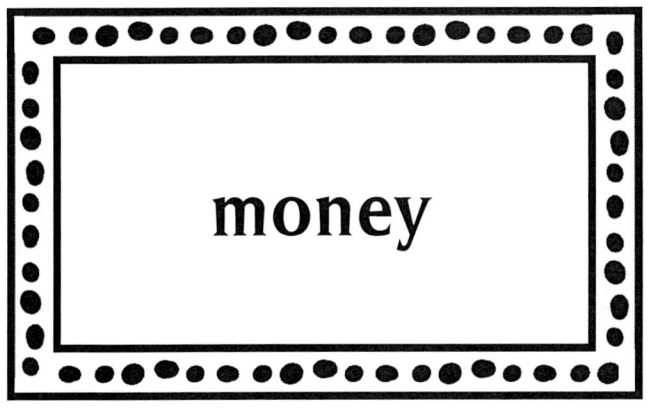
money

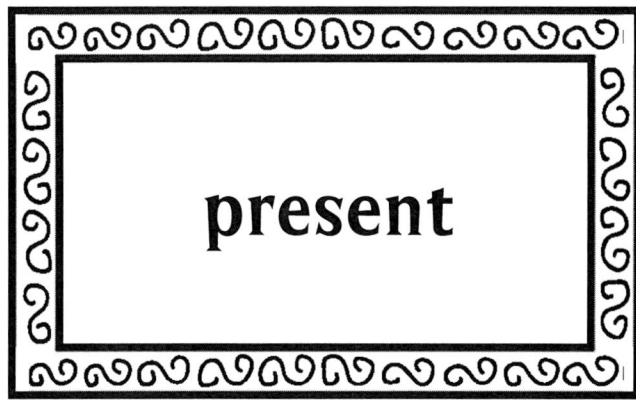
present

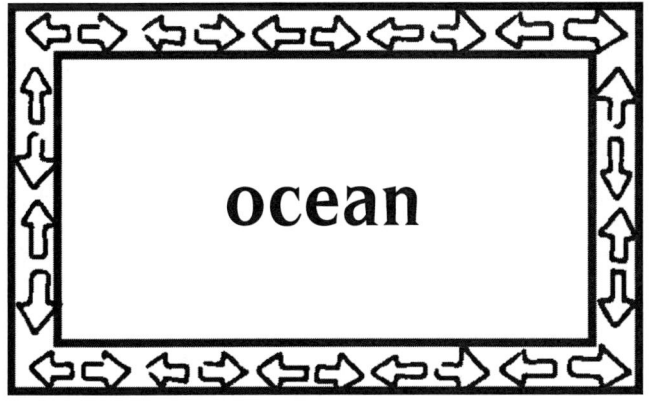
ocean

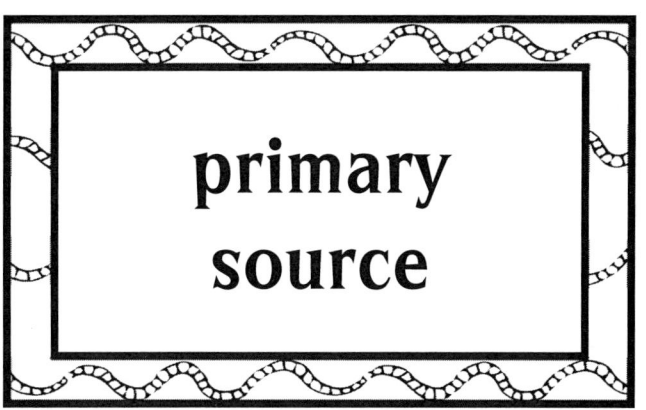
primary source

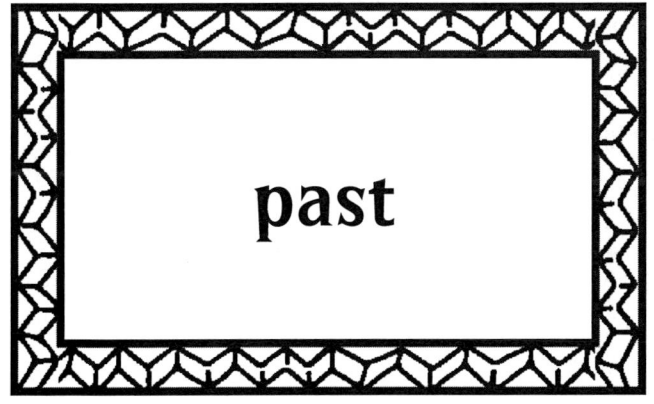
past

producer

VOCABULARY (side 2)

showing love, loyalty, and respect for your country	a shape or feature of Earth's surface
the period of time occurring now	something (such as coins or bills) used as a way to pay for goods and services
a record of an event made by a person who was there when the event occurred	a large body of water on Earth
someone who makes goods or provides services	the time before the present where events have already happened

VOCABULARY (side 1)

responsibility

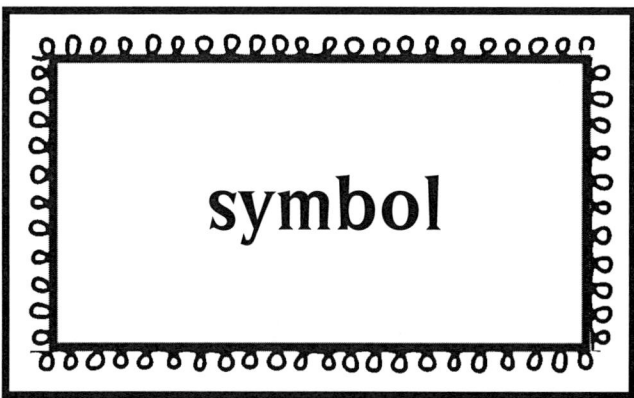
symbol

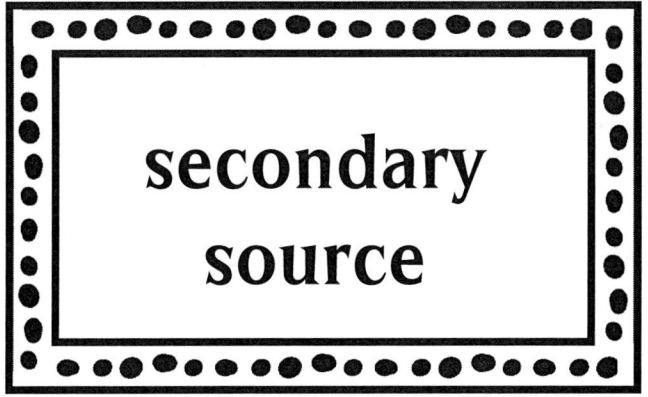
secondary source

timeline

settler

tradition

services

transportation

VOCABULARY (side 2)

a picture or thing that stands for something else	something that is your job or duty to deal with
a table listing events in the order they happened	information about an event that was created later by someone who was not at the event
a belief or custom handed down from one generation to another	a person who settles in a new colony or moves into a new country
all the methods people use to move themselves and their goods from one place to another	activities people do for other people, like cutting hair or repairing a car